BECAUSE IT IS WRONG

BECAUSE IT IS WRONG

Torture, Privacy and Presidential Power in the Age of Terror

CHARLES FRIED

AND

GREGORY FRIED

*l'abbiam fatta tutti noi**

W. W. NORTON & COMPANY

New York • London

For information about permission to reproduce selections from this book,
write to Permissions, W. W. Norton & Company, Inc.,
500 Fifth Avenue, New York, NY 10110

For information about special discounts for bulk purchases, please contact
W. W. Norton Special Sales at specialsales@wwnorton.com or 800-233-4830

Manufacturing by Courier Westford
Book design by Ellen Cipriano
Production manager: Anna Oler

Library of Congress Cataloging-in-Publication Data

Fried, Charles, 1935–
Because it is wrong : torture, privacy and presidential power in the age of terror /
Charles Fried and Gregory Fried.
p. cm.
Includes bibliographical references and index.
ISBN 978-0-393-06951-8 (hbk.)
1. Torture—Moral and ethical aspects. 2. Terrorism—Prevention—Moral and
ethical aspects. 3. United States—Politics and government—Moral and ethical
aspects. I. Fried, Gregory, 1961– II. Title.
HV8593.F75 2010
172'.2—dc22

2010019096

W. W. Norton & Company, Inc.
500 Fifth Avenue, New York, N.Y. 10110
www.wwnorton.com

W. W. Norton & Company Ltd.
Castle House, 75/76 Wells Street, London W1T 3QT
1 2 3 4 5 6 7 8 9 0

---

* "And so it happened that when attempts were made to ask them which work was made by Annibale, which by Agostino, and where Ludovico had lent a hand, nothing could be got out of them but the words: 'It's by the Carracci. We all of us made it.'" Anne Summerscale, *Malvasia's Life of the Carracci: Commentary and Translation* (University Park: Penn State University Press, 2000), p. 148.

Dedicated to the memory of
Leszek Kolakowski (1927–2009)
and to
Samuel, Jonah, Nicholas, Eliza, and Allegra

CONTENTS

LIST OF ILLUSTRATIONS

PREFACE

This is a book born of conversations. Those conversations began between a father and son in the days and weeks after 9/11 and continued on into the years that followed. One of us had been a supporter first of John McCain, then of George W. Bush in the 2000 election. The other certainly was not. One of us supported the war in Iraq, the other only reluctantly. But we were both angered and worried by the 9/11 attacks, and our conversations increasingly focused on two controversial tactics in the war against the terrorists—brutal interrogations of suspected terrorists abroad and pervasive electronic surveillance at home—tactics used to get desperately needed intelligence about a hidden and unfamiliar enemy. Both divided opinion in this country. What we realized they shared is the question of whether an executive has the right to break the law in a time of crisis, for both were indeed illegal. The public controversy about these tactics continues, as does the controversy about what to do with those who ordered and carried out what surely were crimes.

Those are the things we talked about. The questions are timely; we soon discovered that the issues they raised are timeless. The father, a law professor, and the son, a philosophy professor, each had occasion in their lectures, their classroom discussions, and their writing to carry on those conversations with many other participants and audiences. In the spring of 2008, after we participated in panel discussions together at Suffolk University in Boston, we realized that these conversations might become a book that we could write together.

Although both of us have written on ethics for academic audiences, we made it our goal in this book to write for a general audience. We did so because we believe that what is at stake is who we choose to be as citizens of a republic. Though today we are liable to forget it, ours is a nation founded in philosophy; the founders were steeped in philosophical debates over the basis of law and rights, and they respected their fellow Americans well enough to frame the founding documents and Constitution in the terms of those traditions. We believe that we as a nation now face challenges to our founding ideas as serious as at any time in our history. The conversation, therefore, should be as wide as possible and not confined by the narrow habits of scholasticism.

At the heart of the questions we address in this book is one of the major approaches to ethics in the philosophical tradition. Although it goes by a technical name, *deontology*, it represents the way many people respond—and always have responded—to ethical questions in ordinary life. *Deontology* comes from the Greek *deon*, "it is necessary," "it must be done." An ethics based in deontology lays down commands: it says that we must do a certain thing for no other reason than because it is the right thing to do, and it commands that we *not* do other things for no other reason than because they are wrong. For deontology, the standard of action is not that the result of a particular act may be good or bad, but that the act itself, apart from any consequences, is inherently right or wrong. The opposing way of thinking is also familiar and goes by the technical names *consequentialism* and *utilitarianism*. It argues that no act is inherently right or wrong in itself and that the standard of right action must always be the net good produced and the net evil avoided.

While we do not make the contrast between these two approaches at the theoretical level the centerpiece of this book, we should candidly tell you that both of us have, in our respective work in moral and political philosophy, generally supported a deontological position. We have tended to believe and to argue that some acts and institutions are wrong, and others are right, simply because of the kind of acts and institutions they are. We also believe that the founding philosophy of our republic, with its insistence on inalienable rights and sacred duty, is grounded in deontological principles, in particular, the respect for the human being as having a liberty and a dignity that must not be violated by states or individuals, at least not without cause, and even then, only within limits.

We must also acknowledge something else, something that has haunted our conversations since 9/11: the recognition that, at least as a matter of historical fact, our commitment to absolute principles has faced enormous pressure in the years of war that followed the attacks on New York and Washington. In fighting our present enemy, we as a nation have pushed up against the limits of our commitment to norms that we had previously taken for granted. Torture: can it be justified to prevent catastrophe? The violation of privacy: might it be necessary in an age when hyper-technologized systems of information and communication can be used to plan attacks? A presidency unbound by law: is that what we need to respond flexibly and effectively to extraordinary and unanticipated threats?

In addressing these questions, we believe that it would be bad faith to pretend that our traditional sense that some things are simply wrong has not been pushed to its limit. This is not to say from the outset that we must capitulate to that pressure, but we must take it seriously, we must think it through. We wanted to write a book for fellow citizens, and particularly for those engaged in public service, be it in the military or the government, who find themselves running up against those limits in the crises we now face and may continue to face in new and unexpected forms. It does no one any good to pretend that we are not confronted with decisions that go to the very foundations of the republic, even if the dust and fear of 9/11 have seemed to settle and the battle lines pushed back to Iraq, Afghanistan, and other regions even more remote from our everyday lives.

The fervent mixture of panic and patriotism that defined the months after 9/11 have since faded into a resigned sense that we face a long, planetary struggle against an elusive enemy. But we must not allow the inertia of war to prevent us from confronting what we are doing and becoming. While we make an argument and defend it here, we do so in a spirit that recognizes the enormous burden on those responsible for actual policy decisions. But in the end, in a democracy, that is all of us, and so we all must take responsibility for what we now do and become as a nation.

While this book is concerned with the policy issues of our day, we have attempted to address these in terms of principles and debates that transcend the moment, and so in making our case, we have not tried to advance a brief for what detailed policies should be implemented, or which public official should be prosecuted or lionized. Our aim is to make the questions as vividly difficult as we have found them to be, even as we try to answer them, and to provoke all those committed to free, republican forms of government to deliberate about them carefully. Because the stakes are high, we hope to include as many fellow citizens as possible in conversations that began privately, now nearly a decade ago.

CHARLES FRIED
GREGORY FRIED
Boston and Cambridge, Massachusetts
January 2010

BECAUSE IT IS WRONG

INTRODUCTION

INTERROGATION I, BY Leon Golub, shown in the new Broad Contemporary Art Museum in Los Angeles and reproduced here, is a large (ten by sixteen feet) painting in grimly muted colors. It shows a naked man hanging by his feet from the ceiling, his hands tied behind his back. On either side of him stands a jackbooted soldier, one of whom holds a truncheon, poised to strike the body before him. The faces of the two soldiers are business-like, indifferent. The victim's face is indistinct because his head is bent backward and his teeth clenched in pain. As we think about our nation's response to the terror attack on 9/11 and the threat of more, we cannot get this picture out of our minds. It haunts us when we read debates about whether we should once again use what are called harsh or "enhanced" interrogation techniques, whether in the toughest cases the CIA and the military should ignore the Geneva Conventions forbidding cruel, inhumane, and degrading treatment of prisoners.

As in any war, intelligence is crucial, but all the more so in the war with terrorists, because governments know so little about where the enemy is or even who he is. Governments interrogate to fill this gap in their knowledge. With harsh interrogation techniques they seek knowledge by force, but, as in all wars, they also seek knowledge by stealth. This has given rise to another complementary debate: whether the president may authorize the use of supercomputers run by the National Security Agency (NSA) to scan cyberspace for hints and clues about suspicious activity. When these computers pick up certain words, or certain sequences of words in e-mails or spoken messages, or certain words or addresses that appear soon after a certain event, they zoom in to check those messages. They work on algorithms much like search engines do. In this way they pick several hundred thousand communications from the tens of millions in cyberspace. These are then winnowed down further until a manageable number are chosen for inspection by hundreds of clerks in offices of the NSA or FBI or CIA. It is from these that clues to terrorist plots or to the whereabouts of wanted terrorists or criminals might be gleaned. President George W. Bush authorized this warrantless surveillance of cyberspace because there was no way to obtain a warrant for the first or second or maybe the third level of zooming in because there was no known target. The whole point is to discover targets in much the same way that police officers—perhaps in plain clothes—would roam railroad stations or airports looking for suspicious activity, which they would then follow more closely to see if there was anything that needed to be prevented.

This second debate about governments' search for knowledge by stealth also brings a picture to mind: this time it is the picture of Stasi Captain Gerd Wiesler in the attic of an East Berlin apartment house listening to the sounds of his targets making love in the German film *The Lives of Others*.[1] But, of course, what the NSA is doing is not really like that at all, and maybe what the CIA has done to its handful of "high value" captives is not like what is shown in Golub's painting either—although it may come closer: remember waterboarding and the photos from Abu Ghraib.

The debates about these two fronts in the "War on Terror" have gone on in weirdly legalistic terms, perhaps because in one way or another they have come into court and been taken over by the lawyers on both sides. The lawyers ask if the rules of Common Article 3 of the Geneva Conventions apply to the treatment of illegal combatants; and if they do apply, may the president, as part of his overriding duty to protect the nation from attack, ignore them? And the same sorts of questions are asked about the NSA's warrantless scanning of cyberspace: does such scanning violate the Constitution's rule forbidding unreasonable searches (the Fourth Amendment); whether it does or not, did Congress forbid it when in 1978 it passed the Foreign Intelligence Surveillance Act (FISA) in response to the Watergate scandal; and if Congress did forbid it, may the president—once again—direct the intelligence agencies to ignore FISA and even the Fourth Amendment as part of his overriding duty to protect the nation from attack?

Perhaps it is unavoidable that in our lawyer-ridden society these questions get argued out in technical legal terms about the meaning of particular texts, their application to this or that official, the powers of this or that officer of government. But as ordinary citizens, as human beings, we must ask ourselves a deeper set of questions: how should we treat each other, what should we do to those who threaten us, and are our leaders bound by the same rules as the rest of us? Or because they are responsible for all of us, may they do things (and order things to be done) that the rest of us must not?

The two signal controversies of the last several years—torture and eavesdropping—show how far removed from the basic human questions we have come in our debate. We speak as if the two actions were the same, as if a president's involvement in both called for the same kind of condemnation, or could be excused or justified in the same terms. But they are hugely different: perhaps eavesdropping is wrong only because it is illegal. Even if a decent society must draw some lines to protect the privacy of its citizens, few would deny society the authority to intrude almost anywhere with the proper warrant and supervision. Torture is different. Torture is illegal because it is wrong. Look again at Golub's painting. "God created man in his own image, in the image of God created he him" (Genesis 1:27). That is the image of God that hangs between the two jackbooted officers.[2]

ABSOLUTELY WRONG

Think what it means to say that torture is absolutely wrong. It is the word *absolutely* that makes you hesitate. There is no great difficulty in seeing that torture is bad because pain is bad; by itself and without some explanation, some justification, some further story, pain is something no sane person wants for himself or others. And so to cause pain deliberately without justification or explanation is also bad—and no explanation or justification that does not acknowledge that pain is bad is acceptable. Maybe the explanation is that the person to whom you cause pain deserves it as a punishment, or that it is a necessary part of some medical procedure to help that person recover health and functioning or maybe get over a greater pain. So the pain that goes with surgery is justified and what the surgeon does is not bad at all. But all such explanations acknowledge that by itself human suffering—or animal suffering too, for that matter—is bad in itself, intrinsically bad. To say torture is *absolutely* wrong, however, is to say that no explanation, no purpose or outcome can justify it. If torture is absolutely wrong, nothing can make it anything but wrong and nothing can make what the torturer does anything but wrong. Recall Golub's painting. What is being done to that man must not happen—ever, for any reason. That is the claim we examine.

In the last decades many thinkers have given careful attention to the subject of torture, and almost none could bring themselves to conclude that "no exceptional circumstances whatsoever . . . may be invoked as a justification for torture," that torture is absolutely wrong.[1] Usually the author will make an exception for grave emergencies, in which torture might be necessary to head off some great evil. The staple of this literature is the so-called ticking-bomb scenario, in which a bomb—perhaps a nuclear bomb—has been hidden somewhere and will cause immense carnage if it goes off. A terrorist who knows where the bomb is hidden is captured, and he is tortured to make him reveal the hiding place in time to head off the disaster. That case is made up. But there was a real case in which a policeman threatened the kidnapper of a teenage boy with torture unless he told where the boy was confined.[2] The kidnapper readily gave in, but the boy was already dead. The most common strategy is to admit that in principle torture would be justified in such cases, but that in practice the would-be torturer could never be sure enough that this was the right man, or that torture was the only way to get the necessary information.

These arguments try to have it both ways: torture is never justified, but then in some cases it might be justified after all, and the reconciliation of these two positions by supposing that the justifying circumstances will never come up is unconvincing. Of course we can never be completely certain that the justifying circumstances obtain, but that cannot be the standard. When a man kills in self-defense, he cannot be absolutely certain that something less would not save him; when a surgeon amputates a limb, he might not be absolutely certain that this was the only way to ward off gangrene and death. To insist on that measure of certainty to justify torture is to make it an absolute without admitting it. The same objection applies to those who would save torture for cases where many lives are at stake—that is the point of ticking-bomb scenarios. But this too is an equivocation. If averting the death of many people would justify torture, we must ask how many, and does the required degree of certainty go down as the number of potential victims rises? Many incline to think that torturing the kidnapper is sufficiently justified, and do not require that there be hundreds or thousands of lives at stake to get to that conclusion.

And finally, does it matter if the person to be tortured is not the one who created the threat? The usual ticking-bomb or even the kidnapper case supposes that the person to be tortured created or contributed to the threat. But the person who created and can defuse the threat may be peculiarly impervious to pain or beyond reach, but his wife and child may not be. If the number of victims or the certainty of the danger can make a difference in our judgment about torturing the perpetrator, why would we stop short there? The line that is drawn to protect the innocent wife and child is the kind of absolute that most people would hesitate to draw around all torture. But if circumstances can justify the one, why are there not some circumstances dire enough to justify the other?

We propose an argument that the two cases are the same

in the other direction: they are both absolutely wrong—no matter what—and the intuition that protects the innocent wife and child extends to the terrorist and kidnapper as well. It is not an easy argument to make—which is why it makes so many serious people squirm. Before we go on to make it, it would help to consider a line of analysis, call it the institutional analysis, that makes a great deal of sense out of both sides of the intuitions: that maybe torture is not always absolutely wrong, but even so we must never allow it.

Start with a suggestion that law professor, criminal defense lawyer, and civil libertarian Alan Dershowitz makes: in extreme cases, because torture will in fact be used, it should only be allowed if the authorities explain the necessity to a judge, who then issues a warrant that sets out the limits of what may be done.[3] Instead of acknowledging the ingenuity and honesty of the proposal, many commentators—among them those who are unwilling to affirm either that torture is absolutely wrong or that it is sometimes justified—claim to be horrified by it. Richard Posner, a federal judge and professor, does not hide behind ambiguity: he coolly opposes the idea because he thinks that it might lead to more frequent, even routine, use of torture as the Dershowitz warrant becomes bureaucratized, much in the way that search warrants are issued routinely and without much thought by judges and magistrates today.[4] Maintaining the façade of illegality in all circumstances, Posner believes, will more effectively limit torture to the truly extreme and extraordinary situations in which Posner does not hesitate to say it should be used.

Others are not so thoroughgoing in their analysis as either Dershowitz or Posner. The general tenor of the criticism is that torture warrants—and by extension any formal authorization of torture under any circumstances—would represent a debasement, a pollution of the forms and instruments of justice. How awful it would be to have an official manual setting out the exact kinds and degrees of torture, or a training course in torture techniques with certain officials designated as authorized torturers. But if Dershowitz is right in that this approach would minimize the use of torture and confine it to the cases in which it should be used—and remember that these critics are not quite prepared to say there are no such cases—then why be squeamish about the manuals, courses, and certifications? Indeed such squeamishness would be not admirable but reprehensible.

Legal philosopher Jeremy Waldron comes closest to the absolute position. His subject is not why torture is absolutely wrong so much as why admitting it into our law—as Dershowitz's torture warrants would, even if only in rare and extreme cases—would contradict a basic premise, a grounding commitment, what Waldron calls an archetype of a decent, liberal democratic system:

> Law is not brutal in its operation. Law is not savage. Law does not rule through abject fear and terror, or by breaking the will of those whom it confronts. If law is forceful or coercive, it gets its way by nonbrutal methods which respect rather than mutilate the dignity and agency of those who are its subjects.

Waldron understands that often the law makes citizens do what they do not want to do. And if they resist, it may force them to do it, or it may even put them in prison. But

> even when this happens, they will not be herded like cattle or broken like horses; they will not be beaten like dumb animals or treated as bodies to be manipulated. Instead, there will be an enduring connection between the spirit of law and respect for human dignity—respect for human dignity even in extremis, where law is at its most forceful and its subjects at their most vulnerable.[5]

Let us grant that letting torture into the canon of the law means that a legal system could no longer claim that law, even if at times it must be forceful or coercive, never "gets its way by nonbrutal methods"; the legal system could no longer claim that its methods always "respect rather than mutilate the dignity and agency of those who are its subjects." But why must what Waldron calls brutality everywhere and always be beyond the pale; why is the avoidance of some great, perhaps brutal evil never worth the use of brutal means? If brutality is sometimes justified after all, then the argument becomes about whether the law should acknowledge that fact—explicitly, as Dershowitz would, or tacitly and after the fact, as Posner argues.

And so we are driven back to the need to consider whether torture is absolutely wrong. We might suppose that Waldron assumes it is, but that is not his point: his point is that whatever good torture may do, it must never be allowed to become part of the law. And it is a further challenge to discover whether an intuition that torture is absolutely wrong can be explained more fully than by deploying roughly equivalent terms such as *brutality* and *human dignity*. Without more, such terms do not quite amount to explaining the obscure by the more obscure, but they do move in a circle of epithets, appealing to but not illuminating the intuition at the center of that circle. In the end, the appeal of Waldron's argument is like that of the argument that the use of torture sets a bad example. Certainly casual or sadistic torture sets a bad example because it *is* a bad example, but perhaps it is the refusal to use torture in the ticking-bomb or kidnapping case that sets the bad example, a bad example of sentimentality and squeamishness prevailing over the difficult imperative to use distasteful means to preserve a larger human value.

We accuse Waldron of being merely evocative in his use of words to describe torture: *brutality*, *breaking the will*, *mutilating the will*, and *dignity of the victim*. Have we done much better in confronting the reader with Golub's painting *Interrogation I*? A picture may be worth a thousand words, but if the thousand words are all like those used by Waldron, then we too have not moved beyond rhetoric to demonstration. But Waldron and we point beyond metaphors and images to an argument. The words Waldron uses and the picture we offer do point beyond an intuitive reaction to the truths that support the intuition.

We ended the introduction by saying that in Golub's painting it is the image of God that hangs between the two jackbooted officers. The image of God demands reverence, but here the torturers arrange it in a posture of pain and humiliation: the nakedness is not that of a statue of a Greek athlete but of a living carcass, a side of beef ready to be flayed and butchered. The head does not look out serenely and commandingly but is drawn back in agony, the jaw clenched in pain. Then, as the rod is drawn back ready to strike, this body is about to be damaged, the bones smashed, the broken skin made to stream with blood, and the repeated blows causing the victim to lose control of his bowels and bladder, streaking his body with filth. Golub's is a modern, more horrible image than those of the martyrdoms of the saints (Titian's St. Lawrence on the grate) or the horrifying flagellations of Christ depicted by Caravaggio and set out at the head of this chapter. Piero della Francesca's painting *The Flagellation* is a remarkable contrast to these. The flagellation is set in the background and the stance of all the figures is calm, almost decorous.[6] In all of these images the face and body of the victim are those of a human, the image of the Son of God, and the torturers are doing everything they can to make this perfect human ugly, repellent, lacking in control and intentionality, an object only, and on the way to destruction. It is as if a great painting or statue were deliberately defaced, daubed with indelible filth, the marble chipped and broken, the bronze dented and punctured.

These concrete manifestations of abstract, general terms such as *brutality* and *assault on dignity* are the beginning of an account of what those abstractions come to, why they are intrinsically bad, and the start of an explanation of why what we see in Golub's painting is not just intrinsically bad but absolutely wrong, why it is something that must not be done *no matter what*. By *intrinsically* bad, we mean something that is all by itself undesirable, like pain, but the badness may be overridden for a good enough reason—for instance, the pain that might accompany a medical procedure. By *absolutely* wrong, we mean something that can never be right no matter what the circumstances or consequences. What is of intrinsic value may, at times, be sacrificed for other decisive values through a contextual, prudential calculus; what is absolute must not be.

Leon Golub painted *Interrogation I* in 1980–81; the title seems deliberately generic, as if challenging us with the indeterminacy of the location, the context, and the identities of the interrogators and their prisoner. A viewer today, in 2010, might wonder, "But is this prisoner guilty of something, or is there some secret he knows that his interrogators should or even must discover?" Those questions point to a degradation of moral intuition. The viewer asking such questions has become unable to see what Golub depicted as a horror pure and simple, and thereby failed to meet the artwork's challenge. For such a viewer, the painting itself, in a darkly ironic mimicry of the interrogated figure, has become suspended in the torment of ambiguity: is this man a guilty criminal or an innocent victim? Only with an answer to this question of guilt, then, does such a viewer know how to respond morally to the ambiguous horror of the scene. If you need to know, or want to believe, that the man is guilty or possesses some vital information, and therefore in some sense deserves his torture, then the image becomes perhaps no more awful than the depiction of a particularly gruesome form of surgery.

But our contention is precisely that innocence and guilt are irrelevant to torture, that it should not even occur to us in the first place that guilt or information could be a consideration, and that there is no ambiguity in what is being violated here: the image of God.

The human person as the image of God makes two points. By invoking God it points to something not only of transcendent value but of infinite value, of a value and significance than which nothing is greater. And it says that the human person as we see him in his physical manifestation, even one as abject as the victim in Golub's painting, has something of God in him. We spoke of the analogy of torture to the defacing of a great painting or sculpture. The idea is that the painting is not just an abstract manifestation of value; the object itself embodies that value—it is the value. And so in destroying the work one destroys the value itself. And the human form is such a work. No one would claim that the value of a work of art, though intrinsic and not an instrument for anything else, is absolute, but the transcendent nature of God is present in the human form, and so its value is transcendent, beyond price: absolute. But the religious references are not necessary to the point, for humanists have similarly celebrated the sacredness of the human person.

> What a piece of work is a man, how noble in reason, how infinite in faculties, in form and moving how express and admirable, in action how like an angel, in apprehension how like a god! the beauty of the world, the paragon of animals.[7]

Nothing is lost in the logic of our argument (though perhaps something of its force) if we substitute the humanist for the religious conception of this sacredness.

That some things have intrinsic value is not surprising. Were it not so, everything we value we would value on the way to or because of something else, and that is a line we have to get to the end of. Is there just one thing at the end of that line? If, as seems reasonable, there are several—maybe many—things we value for their own sake (intrinsically), then what if these things conflict with each other, as sometimes they must? Either they can be directly at war with each other in particular circumstances, or it may just be that if we seek more of one, then we must accept less of another. We preserve natural beauty in our national parks, but feeding and educating our children may demand spending less on parks or even allowing farms and oil wells to encroach on them. It is not convincing (or even helpful to our thinking) to have some abstraction such as pleasure, happiness, or utility at the end of the line, so that all intrinsic values are valued as they contribute to that one abstract value—much in the way that money might be taken as the supreme value, and everything else is valued as it is translated into money. And that way all questions of conflict and priority are resolved. It is not helpful because pleasure and utility and happiness are so abstract that to resolve conflicts in terms of them is just another way of saying that there is a conflict and it must be (or has been) resolved somehow. Such abstractions do not lead to a solution; they announce it.

In some ways God may be like happiness or pleasure or

utility, in the sense that more concrete, familiar, and immediate goods and values do not translate readily into this ultimate value, and so God cannot easily be invoked to resolve conflicts and establish priorities—unless we somehow determine that God wills some schedule of priorities, which is a solution that depends on our having access to such a divinely established codification. But this objection misses the force of the "image of God" appeal. In Genesis 9:6 we read that "whoever sheds man's blood, by man his blood shall be shed; for in the image of God He made man." Passing over for the moment the use of this passage as a justification for capital punishment, the image of God is invoked to explain a prohibition: to kill a human being is to attack the image of God; as the image of God is inviolable, so are we.

The argument proposes not a scale of values to be pursued, a schedule of priorities, but a prohibition. And it is in the nature of prohibitions that unlike positive injunctions to do this or to pursue that good, they need not conflict with each other. Defacing the image of God is something we must not do, whatever else we do. In rational-choice parlance, this is not a goal to be pursued but a constraint on how goals are pursued. The constraint does not order our goals; it is consistent with any number of plans, projects and orderings, so long as these are pursued while respecting that constraint. To be sure, respecting that constraint respects a value that underlies the constraint, but it respects it in a particular way: it can be a very powerful form of respect in that it may demand giving up some very important goals, but it also leaves us free to pursue whatever goals we wish within that constraint.

Think about lying. The prohibition on lying does not tell us what we may say, or whether we must say anything at all. We may speak nonsense, tell jokes, recite poetry, expound scientific propositions, (truthfully) destroy reputations, all so long as we do not lie. There are values and priorities among all these different instances of speech, but whatever they may be they all play out within the limits of the prohibition against lying. In this sense respect for truth becomes a special kind of value, standing in distinct relationship to all those other values. We do not respect truth by saying as many true things as possible (so that if we say enough true things, it may excuse the occasional lie). That is not it at all. We show respect for truth by not lying.[8] And this constraint may be an absolute constraint: do not lie, ever, no matter what. Or it may be a qualified constraint. Some qualifications are qualifications of degree: do not lie unless something very important is at stake (and the lie is only a small departure from truth, whatever that means). And some are qualifications in kind: do not lie except where the person to whom you lie has no right to the truth, as where even silence will tip off a killer in pursuit of his victim, or as where a host presses his guest about the quality of the food he has been served. The prohibition against killing is in this sense absolute in degree: if the clause "by man shall his blood be shed" is not just a prediction but a permission, then killing of those who have not killed is absolutely forbidden.

So we come back to Golub's *Interrogation I* and the image of God. What kind of prohibition is implicit in the prohibition against beating the hanging man with a truncheon until his bones are broken, his face is smashed, and his liver and kidneys are burst and bleeding? To say of the man that he is the image of God is to say that nothing can justify this, no matter how wicked the victim (an absolute in kind), nor how urgent the purpose (an absolute in degree). This is not an argument. It displays a conclusion, but in a way that we can see what we really are saying and that what we are saying is plausible. If, however secular we may be, we have some notion of the sacred, and if a human being is sacred, then it is at least plausible to claim that what is happening in that painting should not be done—not ever, not for any reason. That is what it means to say the human person is sacred. Now for an account of why this is more than just plausible.

If the human person is of such transcendent value, does not saving her from death—the more so in saving our community and even humanity in its entirety from extinction—require acts as horrific as the torture in Golub's painting? No. It invokes a false metaphor to appeal to Darwinian theory or to a survival instinct in individuals, or whole populations. All Darwinian theory teaches us is that the organisms that adapt to survive do indeed survive. It is not that they deem survival good, nor even that they wish to survive—although such dispositions may be conducive to survival. And then again they may not be: since it is not the survival of the individual organism but of its genetic progeny that is at stake, there may be circumstances in which an individual's disposition to procure its own survival might—past a certain point—prejudice the survival of its genetic progeny. Consider bees, which cause their own death when stinging an enemy of the hive. And even genetic survival must not be misunderstood as either a value or a disposition of any individual organism.[9]

The Darwinian tautology—that the organisms better adapted to survival under particular circumstances will, under those circumstances, survive—tells us nothing about the value of survival itself, much less whether there are things more important than survival. Death is terrible, and we may be more terrified by the prospect of the death of our loved ones, or of our nation, than of our own. But surely we also recognize that there are things worse than death. And we must also realize that in this world, all things perish.

> *For all flesh is as grass,*
> *And all the glory of man as the flower of grass,*
> *The grass withers,*
> *And its flower falls away.*
> I PETER 1:24

We may do our best to hold off the evil day for self, family, or nation, but are we honor-bound to do anything and everything in the name of survival, no matter how horrible, if that day must come despite our best—and worst—efforts? Isn't the fixation on survival a form of self-idolatry? If so, there may well be things we should honor more highly than mere existence, and things we should fear more than death, even the death of those most dear.

Yet the concept of survival is regularly invoked to justify crossing lines and disregarding even the deepest values. There is Lincoln's famous question to Congress regarding his

unconstitutional suspension of habeas corpus at the start of
the Civil War: "Are all the laws, but one, to go unexecuted,
and the government itself to go to pieces, lest that one be
violated?"[10] Later in this book we consider Lincoln's actions
as president in our inquiry into a government officer's duty to
obey the law. But his question also illustrates the ambiguity
of the concept of survival. Survival as what, as who? Is there
not more to us than the continuity of living flesh? If there is a
chain of inheritance by which morels evolve into slime mold,
have the morels survived? If a man continues his biological
existence by committing unspeakable crimes and getting used
to it, has he survived as a man, or has the man disappeared
and been replaced by a monster? If a constitutional democracy
becomes a tyranny that terrorizes its neighbors, what exactly
has "survived"? In such cases, does the person or the nation
truly endure, or are they more truly extinguished? It is not
just that we can trace a continuity which allows the judgment
that something or someone has survived. There is the further
question of what has it survived as. So the answer to Lincoln
might be that it is his willingness to disregard that "one law"
that causes the "government to go to pieces."

The argument in Lincoln's rhetorical question is convincing only on the premise that the body of the laws, or
the Union, is more important than the observance of that
particular constitutional constraint. And the answer is by no
means self-evident. The radical abolitionist William Lloyd
Garrison thought that the maintenance of the Union and of
the Constitution were not worth countenancing the moral
horror of slavery even for one day, and he publicly burned

a copy of the Constitution to make his point. On the other side, some thought that literal fidelity to the Constitution was demanded even at the cost of endangering its continued existence as the Constitution of the Union as it then was. These are great political and world-historical cruces, but on an individual level, men and women have often chosen as if continued survival was not worth participating in some horror. And on the grandest scale, one might ask—as the Garrisonians did—what exactly is the entity whose survival is procured at this price? The Constitution, after all, is a system of laws governing a geographical unit and a collection of people. The land will not sink into the ocean nor all the people perish if the Constitution is abandoned. And if they would sink and perish, is it worth everything that this not happen? Not necessarily—you need an argument for that, or at least a commitment. It is plausible that the answer to Lincoln's question, if asked about the beating and mutilation of the prisoner in *Interrogation I*, is yes: the government should go to pieces rather than allow that horror to be perpetrated, even on a single person.

Men and women die all the time of wasting, disfiguring diseases; they are mauled by tigers and brutalized by strangers and relatives. Some of this we could prevent—whether at little or at great cost. Does respect for the sacredness of the individual mean that there is an *affirmative duty* to sacrifice all other goals and pursuits to ward off such an individual catastrophe? That too cannot be, because such an affirmative duty would certainly crowd out all other pursuits, including others having a similarly urgent claim, such as the protection of the environment from rapid and complete degradation. If respect for the sanctity of human life meant that we must prolong each person's life to the greatest extent possible, not only would all our energy and resources—as individuals and as a society—be exhausted on this goal to the exclusion of all others, but we would not even know how to choose between the effort to save a child and the effort to save an octogenarian with multiple illnesses. By the same token there is not an *affirmative* duty to do everything possible to stop all crime, even horrible crimes against persons, or to spend all our resources on policing. We have not just contradicted our initial assertion, because an affirmative duty of such infinite urgency to even one person must necessarily conflict with a like duty to others.

The imperative is not that men and women not die, even that they not die horribly, but that we—you and I—not be the agents of those deaths. We do not insist that you and I must sacrifice our lives and suspend all our other pursuits to stop the horrors detailed in the reports of Amnesty International, only that, at the very least, we not be the agents of those horrors. And as we have argued, that is an injunction we can all obey without necessarily consuming all our energy and displacing all our other goals. We say not *necessarily* because there might be occasions and circumstances in which refusing to be the agents of evil could cost us everything (for example, if you were a soldier, and you were ordered to shoot a prisoner or else your commanding officer would shoot you), but if this were a positive injunction to do everything we can to eliminate such horrors wherever they occur, then this injunction would at most times crowd out all other pursuits, including the elimination of disease, hunger, and illiteracy.

There are those who will not acknowledge the difference between allowing bad things to happen and being the agent of evil: it is the difference between allowing your commanding officer to shoot first you and then the prisoner, and you shooting the prisoner yourself. It is certainly true that to the sufferer the hurt is the same whether you inflicted it or merely allowed it to happen, through the agency of another or perhaps through no conscious human agency at all. It is also true that the moral revulsion against being the active agent of suffering may be quite an effective device for bringing about the reduction of total suffering in the world. But what we affirm is the rightness of that revulsion in itself, and not just as a device foisted upon us by our nature (learned or instinctive), to lead to better results overall. For reflective moral beings it is no explanation for an attitude or belief that it is a benign trick successfully played on us by nature or culture. Once we see some moral instinct as a mere trick, it no longer works and we must decide for ourselves what we think is right on the merits. There are good reasons—and not just a trick—for marking a difference between what we do and what we merely (!) allow to happen when we could prevent it.

The difference has to do with the kind of beings we are, with what it means to be a moral agent, with how we live our lives in the world. The account is a subtle one, and we must be careful not to slip into arguing that respecting the difference, giving emphasis to personal agency, is right because it works out for the best in the long run after all—that would be embracing the trick. Personal agency is crucial because it is necessary to, really an aspect of, our being distinct, choosing, acting individuals. Our lives matter and what we make of them matters. If we were morally obliged at every moment to do only what is best overall for everyone, the notion of the worth of our individual projects would dissolve, disappear. Those projects have worth not only because they are good, loving, beautiful—in short, human—but because they are chosen as ours. If at every turn we must do what is best for the world as a whole, there would be no place for that—except as a form of recreation, allowed only because recreation is good for us and lets us get back to serving all humanity with increased energy. But if we are not responsible for everything in order that we be more intensely responsible for something, and that something is what we choose as our own project, then the evil that we choose, the horrors we commit by our own agency, are all the more charged to our particular account.

The emphasis on the good and bad we do by our own hands leaves us free of many of the demands that the whole world might make on us, but puts an especially heavy charge on how we exercise that agency. The universalist who claims we are bound at every moment to do that which will be best for everyone everywhere imposes on us a diffuse but all-encompassing duty, but in doing so she lifts part of the burden from us for the evil things we do along the away. If painting the ceiling of the Sistine Chapel is a small thing in the grand scheme, then so is deliberately injuring a child (or torturing a suspected terrorist) a small thing in the grand scheme. Personal agency and the individually chosen project place full weight on the act of painting—or of torturing.

In the painting *Interrogation I* we say that the man hanging there is the image of God, and so we affirm that he (any human being) represents what is most sacred, most ultimate in value and goodness. Therefore, to make him writhe in pain, to injure, smear, mutilate, render loathsome and disgusting the envelope of what is most precious to each of us is to be the agent of ultimate evil—no matter how great the evil we hope to avert by what we do. This may seem to some like (merely) an aesthetic judgment and so to be put aside when the stakes are high enough. That once again is a backhanded way of accepting the notion that morality is concerned with only what is best for the universe taken as a whole. The personal-agency view does indeed have a certain aesthetic quality. Some things are just so repulsive, so ugly, that we cannot, must not bear to do them. Why is that merely an aesthetic, not a moral judgment? It is a moral judgment we offer for consideration, with the acknowledgment that this judgment has the look and feel of an aesthetic judgment, but that is in the nature of ultimate moral commitments.

To borrow a phrase from Ludwig Wittgenstein in another context, there comes a point when we hit bedrock and our spade is turned.[11] We do not want to be seen as torturers, and even more so we do not want to know ourselves to *be* torturers. The human form has a worth and divinity we do not want our action, our intelligence to be directed at defacing. This is the kind of judgment—moral or aesthetic or both, take your pick—that men and women live their lives by and may even give their lives for.

The image of God? How much does our account depend on a belief in God as underwriting the abhorrence to the torture pictured in Golub's painting? If it does depend on such a religious commitment, then the force of the account, though perhaps deepened, is very much narrowed. We do not want that, as neither of us is prepared to make (or deny) such a religious commitment; nor do we want the force of our argument to be narrowed in this way or believe that it must be. The "image of God" may be taken as a metaphor for the ultimate value of the human form as it is incorporated in every person.

But do we mean the human form literally—the face and body of every person? As a human and not a religious commitment, that seems oddly limited and particular. The more general—and more familiar—notion is that it is our humanity itself that is ultimate, sacred; whatever makes us capable of understanding and keeping moral commitments is the moral bedrock of our humanity.[12] There are disadvantages to this perhaps overly moralistic account of what it is that binds us to respect our fellow men and women. It is an account that lacks the visceral appeal of the image of God: an exaltation of the person in all his immediacy, and an order to not mar that whole presence.

As we shall see, this humanistic version of the image of God is at once broader, vaguer, but less concrete, and for that reason perhaps it is less compelling. In breadth, it is an account that condemns more than a physical assault on the physical person. Painless injections that alter the moral faculties, endless questioning of a victim kept awake for days on end, threats to things, persons, and causes dear to the victim, lies and tricks—all these may be seen as assaults on the moral faculty while leaving the physical person untouched. Working for the moral capacity conception is this very breadth and abstractness. The image of God depends to a great extent on the identification we feel with a pictured, visible presence, but many things may estrange us from that presence. Differences between some other person and ourselves may make it hard to see the sacred in that person, especially if that other person is now at our mercy and suspected of some terrible crime. Prior afflictions, whether inflicted on him by his present assailants or by sickness or accident, may make such identification difficult or implausible; when we encounter a human being as ravaged as the man in the Golub painting there is a natural human reaction to look away, to walk past, and to deny that we too might be hanging there. But the humanist resists this aversion and asks only whether this is—or was and might be again—a thinking, feeling being, with plans and hopes, judgments and allegiances. If so, then he is our brother, whatever his transgressions, and in assaulting him we forfeit our own claim to respect as thinking, feeling beings.

There are very difficult questions about what in fact we may do to defend ourselves or others from another person, to punish her for wrongs, to work temporary pain or anguish on her for her own good. And the mere statement of a principle does not answer these. In confronting these questions we get a better idea whether we need the force of the image of God or whether a humanistic conception works as well or better to sustain our decency, to restrain the impulse to be brutal in situations of anguish and crisis.

Before we pass to these difficult and sometimes intricate questions, we pause for a moment to reflect on a different puzzle. We write as if the only question is whether a belief in God is necessary to sustain decency, as if we must decide first what we think about God and then what follows from affirming or denying the divine. But there is an argument the other way: that our commitment to decency and the rejection of brutality as absolutely wrong are reasons for a belief in God. Do we abhor brutality because we believe in God, or do we believe in God because we abhor brutality?

BORDERING ON TORTURE

I T IS NOT at all difficult to grasp why desecrating the human form is absolutely wrong if you keep in mind Golub's painting. But there is conduct on either side of that horrible scene that does not lend itself to so unqualified a response. One is killing. Although killing is awful, there are many situations in which it is justified, maybe even required. There is killing in defending yourself or another person from a deadly attack. There is killing in war. And there is the execution of a murderer convicted in a fair trial. Few would say that all of these are also absolutely wrong. But is it not worse to kill a person than "merely" to torture him?

On the other side are all the techniques used to get information from (initially) unwilling subjects that fall short—maybe far short—of torture. Start with confinement prolonged until the prisoner cooperates. Add to this all kinds of refinements and aggravations: sleep deprivation over many days, confinement in close quarters, confinement with no contact with others, confinement in darkened rooms or with unblinking bright lights, or with constant loud music or complete silence, confinement in uncomfortably hot or cold rooms; continuous questioning by teams of interrogators; requirements that the subject sit or stand in uncomfortable postures; manipulations of diet; physical attacks such as kicking, beating, shaking, and slapping; sexual humiliation, exposure, or penetration. Unfortunately, the list is virtually endless.[1] An extreme position against such coercion would condemn any imposition intended to induce cooperation that the subject would not otherwise freely offer.[2] If that prohibition is too extreme, where on the spectrum of unwanted impositions is some moral line crossed? Only at full-throated torture?

These questions force us to come to grips with the question of what it is that makes torture absolutely wrong, what principle stands behind the intuition that we endorse.

KILLING

Torture grossly offends the bedrock premise that every human being is a locus of inestimable value: a being with plans, emotions, rational and aesthetic or spiritual capacities, and the capacity to form relations to other persons. Altogether, we would call these aspects of a person her soul. Torture offends that premise because it distorts, destroys, or impairs the physical envelope that contains, enables, and expresses the person's soul. We will have more to say about that later in this chapter when we consider the other borderland of torture. At this point in the argument we ask how such an imposition as torture on the physical envelope of the soul can be absolutely wrong, but killing, which eliminates the person altogether, might not be.

The clue to an answer lies in the notion of self-defense: situations in which the only reasonably available way to repel a potential lethal assault is to respond in kind. Most people approve a deadly response in those situations; after all, the alternative is to leave the way open to every aggressor and so put in question the sanctity of one's own life. This answer, without further probing, hardly settles the issue. Is my own life so sacred that I may kill to save it—always, no matter what? Think of all the ways that that is a doubtful, even monstrous, general prescription. Modern medicine offers us many actual and fanciful and not so fanciful challenges. May I kill someone—a perfect stranger—so that his organs can be transplanted into me to save my life? May I kill the child of a person who threatens me, if that murder will turn away the aggressor? And moving in the other direction, surely I am not limited to killing in situations in which it is I but not some other perfectly innocent person who is threatened. Maybe the justification is even stronger there, as it is not colored by self-interest.[3] We pass over the many intricacies of these situations to offer the start of an account of our intuitions.

The central image here—as Golub's *Interrogation I* was the central image in the discussion of torture—is that of hand-to-hand combat:[4] two adversaries face each other in a contest of strength, courage and skill. The picture seems hopelessly remote from the realities of killing in warfare—murders casual and planned, sneak attacks and aerial bombing—but it is worth pausing to reflect why even invoking that chivalric model seems to mock the suffering and brutality of those caught up in modern warfare. In a chivalric contest there is equality, respect, an observance of limits, even though the stakes are life itself. We made the point in the previous chapter that survival is not an ultimate value, but how we survive, what we survive *as*, is. A person attacked defends himself even with deadly force because valuing his own life, and ensuring his own survival, accord with respect for humanity—here humanity in his own person.

Imagine that the attacker also believes (mistakenly) that he is under attack. What principle would require a person (the defender) to yield his life when he has not threatened his attacker in any way? It would have to be one that forbids killing under any circumstances. If what is behind that principle is some notion that all human life is inestimably and ultimately valuable and so one may not kill for any reason, then the principle is the mirror image of the one that makes the defender's own survival a supreme value.[5] Both are incompatible with the idea that life is to be used to pursue other ends and projects—used up in pursuing those projects—and the adjudication between aggressor and victim must invoke some principle of justice just as it must when two persons compete for a piece of property. That principle must not be to fight it out and let the best man win. If it were, then physical strength or cunning would determine who was entitled to survive or to pursue his projects, and so would elevate strength and cunning above other aspects of human nature.

A morality of respect between persons—the same morality

so grossly violated in the case of torture—demands that neither force nor stealth decide the inevitable conflicts between individual projects, but rather principles of justice that accord to each person a fair chance to realize his projects, a principle that affirms the moral equality of all. The commitment to respect others as he respects himself exercises a particular influence on the way he pursues all his other projects.

This commitment is what systems of law represent in well-functioning modern societies. But such systems sometimes fail and people find themselves in contests beyond the reach of the law. And even then, when they are beyond the reach of the law, they may not kill or steal, but they may defend themselves when others try to kill or steal from them. It is the aggressors who cross the bounds of fairness. The victims defending themselves neither disrespect the aggressors in particular nor the principle of fairness in general. (An interesting question is whether in *not* defending against the attack, a man would disrespect *himself*.)

The society of nations is a society without a well-functioning legal system. The rules in the society of nations are contested, incomplete and poorly enforced. Mostly, the rule is self-help; only in very recent times—and then sporadically and unreliably—has there been anything like an outside authority to set the rules, adjudicate conflicts according to them, and then enforce its judgment. War is self-help. The war against terrorists is war indeed. But that does not mean anything goes, any more than in a contest between individuals who find themselves beyond the reach of law. Decency, mutual respect and moderation in the exercise of self-defense, whether retail or wholesale, are expressions of humanity. Indeed, because the unwilling are often recruited to fight battles between nations and peoples, "a decent respect to the opinions of mankind" (words from the Declaration of Independence) demands regard for the humanity of others and so for our own humanity even when we fight them in deadly earnest.

This line of reasoning is a skeleton that we clothe by the metaphor of hand-to-hand combat and, in an earlier time, the invocation of the notion of chivalry. Calling to mind knights on beautifully caparisoned mounts, the very word *chivalry* seems unbearably quaint in the context of modern warfare—think of the Air Force captain sitting at a console in Virginia directing a missile strike from a drone in Afghanistan.[6] But there is a germ of an idea here: however lethal and unforgiving, warfare can be made to go on according to rules—rules about fighting in uniform, about respecting the wounded, about the treatment of prisoners. Keeping such rules allows soldiers to think that they are not just killing machines or raging beasts. They fight, but they fight as men and women. They obey commands, but they will not obey commands to kill prisoners or mistreat the wounded—even if it costs them their lives. Even today, professional soldiers in their manuals and journals speak explicitly of the chivalric ideal behind the rules and restraints they observe. Yes, these restraints are often overlooked and soldiers commit gross atrocities. The extreme stress of battle, the daily experience of mutilation and death, often cause whole armies to break out of the bonds of these ideals. Soldiers in the regular German army, and particularly in its officer corps, were initially repelled by the horrors they saw and the horrors they were ordered to commit. That is why Hitler organized a parallel military in the Waffen-SS. In time the regular army's reluctance broke down. And we too have our My Lais and Abu Ghraibs, where the restraints melted away under the pressure of war. This degradation is particularly likely when we fight an enemy who hides behind civilians, takes and tortures hostages, and kills prisoners and wounded enemy. Under such conditions basic discipline becomes heroism, a heroism that rarely wins medals. Yet the same morality that condemns torture also condemns retaliation in kind against all such criminals—and for the same reason.

And what if some extremely brutal and gruesome forms of self-defense are necessary to repel unjust aggression? Before we look at warfare—particularly modern warfare—where aggression and defense are enacted on a vast stage with many actors, and where these questions have most acutely arisen, let us return first to hand-to-hand, single combat. Imagine a man unjustly attacked by an aggressor armed with a pistol. The only weapon the defender has at hand is a bottle of powerful acid. By throwing it in the attacker's face he will surely stop him, causing blindness, disfigurement, intense pain, and after long agony certain death. The defense is different in kind from the aggression: the aggressor would kill and little else; by throwing the acid, the defender not only kills eventually but also makes the victim's remaining life horrible. To take a person's life in any way is to impose on him a great loss. While death is different from other losses in its absoluteness, it is also inevitable since death is part of what it is to live, and so the shooter is only fixing an event that will happen sometime, an end that shadows us from the moment we begin life. The pain, blindness, disfigurement occur *within* the life. What matters most is *how* life is lived, what it means to the live person and to others who live with him. What life is left to the aggressor is beset with pain, his view of the world is extinguished, and the face he presents to the world—and to himself—is awful, disgusting.

And so we are brought back to *Interrogation I* and the image of God. We are like God because of our face and our capacities—while we are alive; after our deaths all that remains of divinity is the memory others will have of us. So killing and death are more like impediments we suffer, the frustration ending our projects. Like all interactions that have that effect, they are a matter of justice or injustice. The defender who shoots an aggressor is like someone who defends property or like a competitor in a business rivalry. The issue is one of justice: who is the aggressor (whose property is it), and is the defense necessary and proportionate to the threat? But disfiguring another while allowing him to live, as in the acid attack or a flesh-tearing, bone-breaking beating, is quite different from killing in self-defense: the defender does not aim to stop an attack by ending the aggressor's life if need be; rather he aims to change the aggressor from a recognizable, functioning person into something degraded yet still alive.[7]

Looming over this whole line of argument is the response that it is all very well to observe these limits, to play according to these rules when the contenders are more or less evenly matched in strength, in equipment, in numbers. But in the logic of asymmetric warfare, the weak, the outnumbered, the poorly equipped must kill and maim civilians, must torment, humiliate, and execute prisoners, must poison wells and use poison gas just to "level the playing field." The logic insists that if you are going to fight against a conventional military vastly superior to your own, then you must accept doing what it will take to win. Or to put the matter more brutally, war and armed rebellion are not games. Adversaries only fight "according to the rules" when that is in their reciprocal interest. They respect enemy prisoners only because they want and expect the same treatment if they are taken prisoner. But if the fight is so desperate that one side is willing to sacrifice the lives and dignity of its own soldiers taken prisoner, or one side is eager to see its whole population—the young, the old, the sick, and disabled—as enlisted in its cause, then adversaries will not stick to any rules, they will not observe any limits in their fight.

This, of course, is the logic of terrorists. But it misunderstands the argument we have been making. Ours is not a balance-of-power, balance-of-deterrence argument. It is not an argument that depends on a tacit contract between adversaries, valid only if (and so long as) both sides think it is in their interest to accept its terms. It is an argument that insists on the limits we must observe if we are to pursue our goals, protect our community and families, seek to assure our own and their survival *as* decent human beings. There is a kind of millenarian thinking that true believers *must* do anything to achieve their goal because after that goal is achieved, *then* is the time to speak of kindness, love, mutual respect: now they must fight in any way they can. And that is what we deny. We have only one life to live and that must end sometime; what counts most is that while we live it we do so as decent human beings. To deny that is to embrace the logic of the torturers—as many have.

The difference between torture and killing brings us closer to understanding the intuitive judgment that torture is absolutely wrong, but leaves hanging the question of what exactly is torture. There are many things that no one doubts are torture so as to fall under absolute condemnation, but just pointing at examples is not good enough. We need to ask what these examples have in common. *Disfigurement* and *desecration* are terms that bring us closer to that understanding, but they are only metaphors, invocations with a certain intuitive resonance—not a theory or an explanation.

Is it torture to shave a man's head, a woman's head, to pull a tooth, to drill a tooth, to apply electric shocks that cause great pain but do no lasting damage? What of mistreatment that seems to involve no pain but only disorienting discomfort: long periods of isolation (perhaps in a darkened room with no way to mark the passage of time), deprivation of sleep for days on end, subjection to heat or cold, being made to stand or sit in uncomfortable ("stress") positions for many hours on end?[8] And what of sexual torture: rape, forced nudity, and other humiliating displays? Or stripping the subject naked and diapering him, so that he must relieve himself like a baby?

All these and more have been inflicted to get information, to obtain confessions, to make the defiant docile, to terrify into compliance others who witness these things. And what of the administration of drugs that temporarily cause anxiety, forgetfulness, or lack of inhibition? Are some or all of these torture, absolutely wrong, and if so how do they differ from prolonged questioning or simple confinement until compliance is achieved?

Finally, if killing in self-defense is permitted, what about the use of weapons and tactics that inflict on soldiers and civilians the same kinds of injuries, pain, and suffering that in other contexts we have seen as torture? For example, in World War II U.S. troops used flame throwers to flush out or burn to death Japanese soldiers sniping from inside the caves on Iwo Jima.[9] And what of the suffering of the victims of the atomic bomb dropped on Hiroshima, as described in Ibuse Masuji's novel *Black Rain*?

TAKING THE GLOVES OFF

After the terrorist attack on the World Trade Center and the Pentagon, and later during the course of the wars in Afghanistan and Iraq, interrogators in the U.S. military and the CIA were instructed to "take the gloves off" in their efforts to get information from persons captured on battlefields or detained as having possible links to terrorist organizations.[10] (The warrantless interception of electronic communications—an almost certain violation of a Watergate-era statute—was another attempt to develop intelligence in response to those events.) From what we have now learned, these officers engaged in many of the practices described in the preceding section—and worse.[11] Waterboarding, in which the subject is tied to a board and either dunked in a tub of water or has water poured on a cloth covering his face so that he feels like he is drowning, is the most infamous of these practices. Waterboarding induces panic and for some the sense of near death, but properly controlled it has no injurious physical effects. Indeed, specialized U.S. troops were subject to waterboarding as part of their training in resisting enemy demands if captured, and it is reported that one Justice Department official asked that he be waterboarded before he would authorize the use of the tactic. It has since been revealed that the waterboarding actually inflicted by the CIA was far more frequent, prolonged, and brutal.[12] And the then–secretary of defense, Donald Rumsfeld, authorizing the practice of requiring a subject of interrogation to stand for up to four hours without a break, is reported to have scribbled a note to the effect that he often has to stand that long.[13] Are all or some of these practices torture?

In Gillo Pontecorvo's 1966 film *The Battle of Algiers*, which portrays the efforts of the French army to defeat the Algerian insurgency's campaign of terror, we meet a modest young Algerian partisan. He is captured by the French, and when we see him again he is leading the soldiers to the secret hiding place of the insurgent leaders, who are bricked up behind a blind wall. As the soldiers batter through the wall, the Algerian's face tells the story of the torture that led him to this betrayal. It is abject, broken: it pleads that he could not help what he has done. He has been unmanned. The techniques the U.S. interrogators used and the repeated denials that they constitute torture force us to go beyond just pointing at clear instances and saying, "It's like that!" The techniques are aimed at getting the victims to do something: to reveal information, maybe (as in *The Battle of Algiers*) to lead their captors to a secret hiding place. But then so is the most correct and restrained questioning. What is the difference between terrifying a captive by repeated bouts of waterboarding on one hand and repeated questioning sessions in ordinary surroundings, with the captive otherwise receiving standard care, on the other? With waterboarding, stress positions, electric shocks, sleep deprivation, and the like, the captor inflicts acute physical distress—usually pain, although waterboarding and sleep deprivation may not inflict pain so much as fear, anxiety, and disorientation. We affirm that all the techniques like waterboarding, stress positions, sexual humiliation, and sleep deprivation are absolutely wrong, whether or not it is worse to beat or mutilate a prisoner than to waterboard or deprive him of sleep.[14]

Here is a first approximation—drawn from the Geneva Conventions and the U.S. Army *Field Manual*[15]—of what distinguishes permissible from impermissible interrogation techniques: those who detain hostile persons in their power must treat them in the same way as they treat their own personnel; detainees must get similar food, shelter, and clothing, rest and exercise, except as may be necessary to prevent their escaping or harming their captors or other detainees. The Army *Field*

Manual section titled *Human Intelligence Collector Operations* proposes all sorts of permissible and possibly effective interrogation techniques. These include pretending to know already the answers to questions, asking the same questions over and over again to trap the subject in contradictions and to confront him with them, falsely stating that other prisoners have already given the information being sought or otherwise have betrayed the cause to which the prisoner is seeking to remain loyal, and alternating between harsh interrogators and friendly ones. But the army's limits on what can be done are very severe and are more detailed than those in the Geneva Conventions. In drawing the line between the permissible and the impermissible, the *Manual* tries to distinguish techniques that seek to influence a person's will from those that seek to destroy it. It is a difficult line to draw at the margins, but let us start at the center of the two territories and move toward their common border.

In the film *The English Patient*, German army intelligence agents interrogate an Allied officer captured in North Africa during World War II. His hand is strapped to a table, and when he proves obdurate, the agent—with a nurse standing by—cuts off a finger of his left hand. Then another. As the interrogator moves to cut off a third, the officer cracks and gives the information demanded of him. The session includes pain, permanent loss, and fear of greater loss.*

---

* In an October 16, 2009, decision the British High Court of Justice (Queens Bench Division)([2009 EWHC 2549]) ruled that its description of the torture suffered by Binyam Mohamed, redacted from the court's earlier judgment at the urging of the Obama administration, should be

Pain undermines a subject's ability to reason. The greater the pain, the more it overwhelms everything else in a subject's spirit.[16]

We can see this happening even with mild pain—a headache. However, we can usually put that to one side and think about other things. Greater pain crowds other things out. The person in such pain just wants it to stop. This is an intrinsically human reaction. The evolutionary function of pain, its physiology, is to compel our attention to a danger and force us to act until it is removed.[17] This functional analysis is, of course, too cool. Pain is completely effective when it becomes unbearable. It is not as if the torturers gently put the subject's mind to sleep and then lead him where they want him to go. Pain operates by making the sensation the strongest, the worst thing he can experience, so that at the moment nothing is worse than that it should continue. This is what we mean when we say that pain crowds out the spirit, and in the extreme, it breaks it altogether so that there is nothing but pain. The contrast to persistent, deceptive, or "good-cop-bad-cop" questioning should now be clear. Those techniques do not break the mind: they appeal to it, they use it, they manipulate it.

The torture in *The English Patient* involved, one might suppose, great pain, but not so great that if it were caused by a toothache or broken limb it might have been borne and the questioner resisted. The torture succeeded not only because

---

made public. The report included descriptions of "how Mr. Mohamed's genitals were sliced with a scalpel and other torture methods." The details had earlier been reported in the *Daily Telegraph*, February 7, 2009.

the officer's vivid perception of the loss of part of his hand disgusted and horrified him to a degree that may have over-whelmed calculation and control, but more than that, because the officer faced another human agent who had him com-pletely in his power, who could do whatever he wanted to him, who was constrained by no sense of human fellowship or pity. Torture victims often do not give up their secrets in the midst of their worst agony—the pain is too great to allow a coherent or reliable statement; nothing but howls of pain are possible. It is between sessions that the victim yields. He might be ques-tioned—perhaps in a room surrounded with the instruments of torture, within earshot of other victims screaming in other rooms—refuse to answer, be tortured, and then questioned again. It is the immediate memory of torment and the threat of its imminent repetition that produce the result. So it was with the English officer in North Africa. One might say that this is a calculation made by the victim, but it is made under a threat so terrible and present that the calculation becomes a mockery of reflection and is experienced as irresistible to the same degree as if the choice were elicited during the agony itself. So torture often works by the threat of torture, made real and irresistible by an immediately past session of torture that the interrogator can repeat. Indeed he may repeat it even before the victim has a chance to respond, just to show how completely the victim is under the unfettered control of the interrogator.

By contrast, interrogation "by the book"—for example, the Army *Field Manual*—not only respects limits but also displays to the subject that those who have charge of him are limited in what they can do. They can offer inducements and remove privileges,[18] and their control is total in the sense that they can threaten indefinite confinement, but the envelope of the person is inviolable: it may not be cut, burned, frozen, or exposed. This is another way of stating the international prohibition on "cruel, inhuman and degrading" treatment.[19] There is observed a modicum of respect between questioner and subject, captor and captive. The last of the three prohibitions, the prohibition against "degrading" treatment, sums it up best. The diapering of grown men and the forced displays of naked prisoners in mock sexual contacts staged for the cameras in the infamous photographs from Abu Ghraib[20] are vivid examples of painless but extreme forms of degradation.

The Bush Justice Department's[21] exegesis of the meaning of cruel, inhuman, and degrading treatment as "conduct that shocks the conscience" is entirely inadequate. The term comes from the 1952 Supreme Court case of *Rochin v. California*.[22] A prisoner's stomach was pumped to retrieve illegal drugs he had swallowed. Justice Felix Frankfurter, writing for a unanimous Court, ruled that a conviction based on "conduct that shocks the conscience" violates due process of law and cannot stand. The standard was also invoked in the 1985 case of *Winston v. Lee*, in which a bullet to be used as evidence was dug out of an unwilling subject.[23] But it is an inadequate standard, because it offers no explanation as to why these instances shock the conscience. If the stomach pumping or bullet retrieval had taken place under anesthesia, would this have shocked the conscience? And what does this standard tell us about waterboarding?

WAR

We have presented torture as a technique for eliciting information or confessions,[24] but it is also used in more generalized ways as punishment or to terrorize and so discourage resistance. Of course, threatening death is terrifying in itself, but cruel death or cruelty even without killing offends respect between persons in a distinct way. The death penalty all by itself takes away life, separating the subject forever and in every way from the human community, but while he lives, the penalty does not try to destroy him as a person. This then leads us to war and the use of terror in war.

At the outset we proposed that killing in self-defense and so in warfare is not always wrong. War is often justified by thinking of it as self-defense on a large scale, and that is why a war of aggression is a moral offense and an offense against the law of nations.[25] (We put aside whether a preemptive strike can be counted as self-defense. In the classic Western showdown, the hero must wait until his adversary unambiguously reaches for his gun before he may beat him to the draw and shoot him; he need not, however, wait until his adversary unholsters his gun, and certainly not until he shoots.) There are very great differences between the paradigm of single combat and modern warfare, and not only the difference of scale. In the latter, the fighting occurs between soldiers who have not personally picked the fight, may not have been attacked, and indeed as conscripts may be unwilling participants with no animosity toward the soldiers they must try to kill or capture. Second, the fighting often reaches the persons and property of men and women who are not soldiers and may not sympathize with or provide support to those who do fight.

Whether opposing soldiers are eager or reluctant to attack you, the threat is the same and so is the right to defend against it. But just *because* the combatants are remote from the initial decisions that make one side or the other the aggressor, the rules about how they should be treated are particularly urgent. The writer Elaine Scarry has invoked the concept of chivalry; when you think about how professionals are to treat other professionals, both under orders, the invocation is not as quaint as it might seem at first. The distance between those who fight, risking injury and death, and those who order them to fight makes it particularly appropriate that the former should be protected by some fairly rigorous rules—like those that protect contestants in a sport in which they have no personal animus but yet at some risk seek to triumph over adversaries. For a commander to order (as German soldiers fighting on the Eastern Front in World War II were ordered) his troops to observe no limits not only disrespects the persons harmed—in combat or as prisoners—but also disrespects his own troops, as if the soldiers on both sides were automata or draught animals to be set in motion, having neither conscience nor judgment of their own.

After the Battle of Princeton in 1777, General George Washington commanded, "Treat [those captured in the battle] with humanity, and let them have no reason to Complain of our Copying the brutal example of the British Army in their treatment of our unfortunate brethren. . . . Provide everything necessary for them on the road."[26] This conception is embodied in the elaborate rules about how prisoners are to be treated, what weapons (such as poison gas and bullets designed to inflict particularly grievous wounds)[27] may or may not be used, what persons—such as the wounded and the medical personnel who treat them—are *hors de combat*. As in much positive legislation, all the particulars cannot be drawn from the principles of humanity and mutual respect (combatants recognizing in each other the image of God) in the way that corollaries are drawn from axioms. But the rules for the conduct of war *are* animated by these principles and have secured from professional soldiers a loyalty that makes their way of life—killing and being killed—seem to them tolerable, and perhaps because of these limits (which put them at risk) even noble. Jean Renoir's film *La Grande Illusion* (1937) illustrates the struggle of soldiers trying to maintain and respect their own and each others' humanity.

The 1977 additional protocols to the Geneva Conventions,[28] and before them the evolving Enlightenment understanding,[29] show great regard for the safety of those who do not fight. Noncombatants do not fit into the scenario of a struggle between two contestants who directly threaten each other. Soldiers on both sides might—rightly or wrongly—believe that they are justified, that it is their opponents who are the aggressors, and the soldiers on both sides might have been conscripted into the fight having no clear convictions of the rights and wrongs of the struggle. But the soldier's children standing by cannot by any plausible extension be drawn into this picture. Nor can the soldier's wife who looks after his children while he is at the front. Nor yet the teachers at those children's school. And not those who deliver food to that school. It is true that threats to any of these noncombatants might discourage the combatants' willingness to carry on, but this cannot stand as a justification for striking (or threatening to strike) them. The use of those who do not threaten harm as a way of defending against those who do offends the paradigm of reciprocal engagement that alone justifies intentional harming of another. (Recall that harming the victim's child is not a more remote but rather a worse crime than harming the victim directly.) Lip service is paid to this principle even today in an era of aerial bombing and long-range artillery, with frequent and perhaps inevitably heavy civilian casualties: Civilians may not be intended as the targets of military action, and even when harm to civilians is claimed to be an unintended though inevitable side effect of the action, the law of war demands that this "collateral damage" be proportional to the intended military goal and that precautions are taken to minimize such collateral damage to the extent possible. This principle of proportionality is at the heart of the controversy about Israel's 2008 military action in Gaza.

Of course, history is full of horrors threatened or carried out against civilian populations. But the same sharpening of moral focus that led to the recognition of the gross immorality of torture (which in earlier times was routinely sanctioned by church and state) has also led in modern times to a firm line being drawn against such practices. In World War II these limits were transgressed on a vast scale, first by the Germans and Japanese but then in Allied terror bombing of German cities, the firebombings of Dresden and Tokyo, and most stunningly by the atomic bomb attacks of Hiroshima and Nagasaki.[30] Although there might have been peripheral military objectives in many of these cases—Dresden was a transportation hub of Axis military movements, Hiroshima had been a port of embarkation for Japanese troops—the avowed aim was to demoralize the enemy populations, breaking their will to carry on.

This categorical judgment assumes there is a clear line between combatants and noncombatants, but in modern warfare there is not. Whole economies are mobilized. Perhaps those who make the arms for the fighters are as much a threat as the soldiers who bear them—remember, neither might have chosen this fight. But what of those who feed both the factory workers and the fighters, and those who feed the feeders? Modern integrated economies and a clearer understanding of how those economies function have made the classical paradigm distinguishing fighter and bystander hard to maintain. The international codes that have been formulated—like all legislation—are approximate and at the margins arbitrary, but they make the effort.[31]

In these three areas—treatment of conscripts, the definition of combatants, collateral damage—the international legislation represents an attempt to embody in precise terms the underlying moral distinctions. Because the legislation is approximate, arbitrary, vague, or all three, there is a temptation to dismiss it as irrelevant. Worse yet, unscrupulous actors manipulate the norms so as to gain advantages while disabling responses by their adversaries. The use of human shields, disguising fighters as noncombatants, and the practice of locating military facilities in civilian areas are frequent examples. We do not propose rules about the appropriate response to such criminal practices. Our point is to show how the norms themselves embody fundamental moral limits, even though what is absolutely wrong is sketched out in concrete rules that speak in such relative terms as proportionality. In responding to evasion and abuse, honorable fighters will remember the underlying values and try to respect them. That is what chivalry demands.

The signers of the Declaration of Independence pledged not only their lives but also their "sacred honor" in the struggle that had already begun. George Washington's command to his troops about the treatment of prisoners illustrates this sense of honor.

THE DEATH PENALTY

In trying to understand what makes torture absolutely wrong, and what is allowed and forbidden in warfare, it surprises us that what we have concluded has implications for the moral permissibility of the death penalty. Although that is not our subject, tracing those implications deepens the arguments about torture and warfare.

The death penalty—especially for the most heinous or threatening crimes—has often been accompanied by prolonged and gruesome torments. These were intended to have both a deterrent and an exemplary effect, as if the body of the condemned were a billboard on which the judgment of his crimes was displayed.[32] In modern times this element has been steadily subtracted from the death penalty. Executions ceased to be public, and the means chosen were meant to be swift and relatively painless. This was the idea behind the guillotine, and even hanging if expertly carried out. Death by firing squad in military executions is meant to preserve the soldier's honor by dispatching him in a way that resembles death on the battlefield. Hanging and beheading (which in England was reserved for noble traitors), though quick and painless, mutilated the body in a way that was felt, at least by analogy, to dishonor the humanity of the victim. This led to more modern means of execution such as electrocution and the gas chamber, although there is considerable doubt as to whether they were quick, painless, or respectful of the body's integrity.

The last step in the United States has been the near-general adoption of execution by lethal injection. Assuming that the procedure really is painless,[33] it has grotesque aspects all its own. It assumes the guise of a medical procedure (it resembles what happens to a patient in preparation for major surgery), while mocking medicine's most basic and ancient injunction to do no harm.

Abstracting from everything about the death penalty except the ending of life makes vivid what the death penalty really is: a live person completely helpless in the hands of his captors is put to death without hope or opportunity of resistance or remonstrance. Much more than killing on the battlefield, it enacts the total subjection and subsequent annihilation of one person by another. All moral equality between executioner and victim is denied. The condemned for that moment exists only to be killed. Worse still, it is not only the executioner who has this total power over the condemned, but society as a whole that has organized itself to kill. The execution does not happen in a flash of unplanned rage. Rather, an elaborate, carefully prescribed sequence leads up to sedating the condemned, strapping the convict to the gurney, inserting needles in veins and then injecting the substances that will kill—all in the presence behind one-way windows of witnesses, often including members of the family of those the condemned person had killed.

Torture enacts one kind of ritual, assaulting the humanity of its victim, tearing his body, overwhelming his consciousness with the worst sensations his tormentors can devise. It does its work by acknowledging human consciousness and sensitivity in order to excite, overwhelm, and destroy it. If a human being is a painting, then torture defaces that image by cutting, fouling, and finally obliterating it. Execution by lethal injection denies humanity in another way. It treats its victim as if he were an inhuman object. The execution not only affirms society's control over the condemned, its right to restrain him and to protect itself, but also enacts society's total ownership of him, maybe even more than it would if its agents tortured him. He is treated as an object to be eliminated, a machine to be decommissioned and disposed of, vermin to be exterminated.

Our self-respect allows us to defend ourselves even to the point of killing. That was the starting point of the discussion in this chapter. Because the condemned, like the torture victim, is immobilized, he does not present an immediate threat. The execution is preemptive; it anticipates and eliminates the need for future defense, but killing is not a necessary way of doing that, only the cheapest and most certain way, which is not enough to justify it. Kant has argued that execution is not only justified but also required as a matter of justice in response to the worst crimes—justice even to the condemned because it holds him responsible for his own actions.[34] In a sense this is true, if the execution is in response to a proven serious crime and not, say, a kind of sanitary measure to eliminate unproductive or even unattractive persons. But the argument begs the question by assuming that execution is the only, the most appropriate response, or an appropriate response at all.

The theory of punishment is not our subject, but it comes to mind because the Kantian constraint of respect for persons figures so prominently in our argument. Punishments deter, incapacitate, and denounce. In all of these roles they visit an undesired consequence on their objects and in that sense use them as means to our collective ends. Justice and mutual respect are the constraints on the use of punishment. Only the guilty can be punished, however much a deterrent it might be to torment the offender's wife or children. We suggest that it is morally wrong to kill a person totally in our power just as it is morally wrong to torture a criminal. Compare the death penalty to life imprisonment with no expectation of release.

The use that makes of, for instance, a proven killer—to keep her from killing again and to announce the heinousness of her crime—at least allows her to live on and to shape the rest of her life in the awareness of what she has done. We continue to relate to her, though in limited ways. We do not assume total ownership of her by eliminating her altogether.

The reciprocity of respect observed in the treatment of captives and criminals was stunningly summed up in an analogous context by Abraham Lincoln: "As I would not be a slave, so I would not be a master."[35]

THE BIG EAR

S EPTEMBER 11, 2001, was a shock. Not since the Civil War had an enemy attacked us and wrought major destruction on our continent. Where before we had felt smugly secure, now we saw that we were vulnerable. That instant sense of vulnerability caused our economy to contract. Systems of ease and confidence were replaced with wary precautions everywhere. We did not even know where the enemy was or even exactly who he was. Suspicion replaced trust. Ordinary citizens, living far from potential targets, felt undermined, threatened, violated. And, of course, that is exactly what terrorists hope to accomplish. An attack on a military target in a war is understandable, in a way even expected. An attack on a bus or train or school or office building shows that any of us might be next. In *The Secret Agent*, Joseph Conrad portrays the heart of terrorists: his protagonists target not a military installation but the Greenwich Observatory because it is a symbol of peace, order, and progress—the place from which Greenwich Mean Time is measured, rather like Sèvres, France, where the standard meter bar is kept. The target is a symbol of normalcy, of dependability; its sturdy everydayness is the reason it is chosen for attack.

And so the twin towers fell, and our society and our government went into spasm. President George W. Bush—till then an amiable man interested in tax cuts and literacy—understood that his first duty was to protect his fellow citizens, ordinary men and women like himself, from further danger. Because no one knew where that danger lurked, information—or rather the lack of it—was the key. By brutalizing, driving mad, and torturing suspected terrorists, our government was neither exacting revenge nor setting a terrible example to deter other terrorists (motives that had moved many regimes to use torture in the past). Its overriding goal was knowledge. Our government wanted the terrorists in its custody to yield up their secrets. And because knowledge was the predicate for protection and the antidote to terror, our government not only tortured to get knowledge out of unwilling mouths by force, but also sought knowledge from willing but unwitting mouths (and pens and keystrokes) by stealth. It eavesdropped—and continues to eavesdrop—to an unimaginable degree on words and signals so numerous that a word was invented to count it. One estimate has it that the volume of information surreptitiously collected and stored will be counted in a few years not in mega- or giga- or even terabytes, but something called yottabytes (10^{24} bits of information); to store this gargantuan stock of information, the government is building city-sized facilities.[1]

Such revelations cause panic and resentment in ordinary citizens. Privacy leagues give the alarm, editorialists warn of vast, unspecified dangers to our liberties, Congress holds hearings and threatens legislation.[2] Although there was (and is) widespread revulsion at the government's brutal treatment of our enemies and suspected enemies—recall the reaction to the Abu Ghraib photographs—there was genuine alarm at the government's big ear. In 2002 the Department of Defense proposed the Total Information Awareness project, the centerpiece of which was an elaborate computer system that would scan information in government and public records—bank, billing, and credit card records and the like—in order to discover patterns and associations pointing to possible terrorist-related activities. The striking feature of this program was not the aspects that might involve prying into records that are otherwise unavailable to the government or the public in general (for instance, to diligent and ingenious news media), but rather the novel technical capability of collecting and collating (mining) this vast array of data for clues and evidence. To quiet the panic, in 2003 the Department of Defense was forced to set up the Technology and Privacy Advisory Committee, charged with advising the secretary of defense on "the protection of personal privacy in the pursuit of technological solutions to identify terrorists and prevent terrorist attacks against the United States."[3] The committee's report forced the abandonment of the project—at least by that name, and (as we discuss in the next chapter) though the administration continued to press for it, it was not until 2008 that Congress authorized some, but not all, of the surveillance activities that the government had engaged in all along.

Another remarkable example of our preoccupation with

privacy came to light in late 2009, just after Umar Farouk Abdulmutallab was caught trying to detonate the powerful plastic explosive pentaerythritol tetranitrate on a flight from Amsterdam to Detroit, on Christmas Day. Abdulmutallab reportedly smuggled the explosive onto the airplane by sewing the material into his underwear. Furthermore, we know that terrorists have gone to greater lengths than Abdulmutallab: an al Qaeda operative carried an explosive in his rectum and allowed a confederate to detonate the device remotely by cell phone in an attempt to assassinate Prince Mohammed bin Nayef, the head of Saudi counterterrorism. Airport security does not allow routine pat-down searches of passengers' groins or inspections of their body cavities, and it would be hard to imagine that ever happening. Such invasive measures might be unnecessary, though, because it turns out there is a new technology, the millimeter wave scanner, that can produce an image that sees through all clothing and even into body cavities. But privacy advocates have protested the deployment of this device and have already advanced legislation to prevent its routine use, because it seems such an intense invasion of privacy.

It is remarkable that no such brake was put on the government-sanctioned torture until several years later, and even now President Barack Obama's director of the CIA has stated that in urgent cases he might once again have recourse to "enhanced" interrogation techniques.[4]

The cynic might say that there is a privacy panic but no torture panic because ordinary citizens do not expect that they or anyone they know is likely to be tortured. But we all fear that the government's big ear may be listening in on even our most intimate whispered conversations, ferreting out our smallest indiscretions, most trivial legal peccadilloes—even though torture is infinitely worse, more brutalizing to torturer and tortured alike, than listening bugs and wires and spy satellites. After 9/11, the government, in its desperate search for knowledge, both tortured and eavesdropped in violation of the law, but it is grotesque to equate the two and to agitate more against eavesdropping than against torture.

Stepping back from intuition and reflex, we may ask, what is wrong with eavesdropping? Privacy! The right to privacy! To invoke these terms is to substitute a slogan for an argument. Where we have worked in the preceding chapters to excite the conscience against our government's use of torture, should we not now deploy mind, heart, and rhetoric to quiet the privacy panic so that government can go about its business of ferreting out the information it needs to protect us?

The most famous defense of privacy is the 1928 opinion of Supreme Court Justice Louis Brandeis in *Olmstead v. United States*, a wiretapping case. He wrote,

> The makers of our Constitution undertook to secure conditions favorable to the pursuit of happiness. . . . They sought to protect Americans in their beliefs, their thoughts, their emotions and their sensations. They conferred, as against the Government, the right to be let alone—the most comprehensive of rights and the

right most valued by civilized men. To protect that right, every unjustifiable intrusion by the Government upon the privacy of the individual, whatever the means employed, must be deemed a violation of the Fourth Amendment.[5]

So put, the concept of privacy is capacious indeed. It is coextensive with all limits on government impositions, and (why not?) all limits on impositions by one person on another. In this way, a punch in the face, a burglary, and excessive tax are all violations of privacy. In fact, this concept of privacy is so capacious that it does no explanatory work. It is simply coextensive with any violation of one's legal or, for that matter, moral rights. And the world has famously taken Brandeis up on his famous dictum. The rights to choose abortion and to engage in homosexual activity have been gathered under the rubric of privacy. The latter, to be sure, usually takes place "in private," but abortions are performed, if not on a public stage, still in public institutions, with all the institutional paraphernalia about them: waiting rooms, receptionists, records, reports, licensed practitioners. If we are to understand, tame, or justify the privacy panic about the big ear, we need a notion more discriminating than Brandeis's "right to be let alone."

Here's a start. Think of the German film we mentioned earlier, *The Lives of Others*:[6] Gerd Wiesler, a captain in the Stasi, the Ministry of State Security, has been ordered by a superior to install hidden microphones in an apartment where Georg Dreyman, an East German playwright suspected of pro-Western sympathies, and his lover, prominent actress

Christa-Maria Sieland, live. In fact Wiesler's superior is bending to the wishes of a government minister who lusts after the actress and is scheming to pry her away from her lover. In a secret listening booth set up in the apartment building's attic, Wiesler listens to everything that goes on in the apartment: meetings with friends, casual conversations, lovemaking, pillow talk. Gradually Wiesler enters into these good people's lives, and his revolt against what he has been asked to do and being made an instrument of the actress's destruction leads to his removal from his post. At the end of the film we see him in present-day Berlin, delivering letters—unopened, unread, unviolated—from his workaday postman's pouch.

The menace implicit in the ubiquitous Stasi system of informants and eavesdropping derived from what the East German state had in store for people who came into its sights: arrests, torture, imprisonment. It is a wild understatement that arbitrary arrest, torture, and imprisonment violate "the right to be let alone." But subtract these horrors and there is still something left that we fear and despise. Consider the biblical tale of the drunkenness of Noah depicted by Michelangelo at the head of this chapter:

> Noah was the first tiller of the soil. He planted a vineyard; and he drank of the wine, and became drunk, and lay uncovered in his tent. And Ham, the father of Canaan, saw the nakedness of his father, and told his two brothers outside. Then Shem and Japheth took a garment, laid it upon both their shoulders, and walked backward and covered the nakedness of their father;

their faces were turned away, and they did not see their
father's nakedness. When Noah awoke from his wine
and knew what his youngest son had done to him, he
said, "Cursed be Canaan; a slave of slaves shall he be
to his brothers."

GENESIS 9:20-25[7]

If we superimpose Wiesler's story on the biblical story
of the drunkenness of Noah and subtract the very modern
aspect of the East German state suppression, what is left is not
the loss of control over our lives but the loss of control over
information about ourselves. What is so distinctly threatening about loss of control over information about ourselves? In
some cases, the control of information is simply instrumental
to having control over a material good itself. A person keeps
her bank account number and personal identification number (PIN) private because she does not want anyone raiding
her money there. She keeps a numbered Swiss bank account
because she does not want the IRS prying into her finances.
But she might not be worried about the IRS or creditors or
identity thieves getting access to her account. She just might
not want any but a few people to know how much money she
has in that account. And that would be a core privacy interest.
She might want to present—or *not* present—a certain face to
the world: that of a rich society woman, or of a person of modest means struggling like all her friends to make ends meet. If
she is very rich, perhaps she does not want people—especially
men—to befriend her because she is rich, even if she is not
worried that they will steal from her.[8]

———

Sensitivity about privacy is a very modern sentiment—perhaps an artifact of our mobile, cosmopolitan, numerous, and anonymous society. In explaining why privacy is celebrated, often in terms as extravagant as those of Justice Brandeis, we confront a paradox. The right seems to begin with a wrong. Even the Latin roots of our English word *private* suggest an inherently negative origin. In Latin, *privus* is an adjective meaning individual, isolated, specific, particular, or one's own. It is something set aside and disconnected, and the verb *privare* means to deprive, to bereave, to rob, to strip—a sense we can still hear in *deprive* and *privation*. And so in Latin, to be *privatus* means to have withdrawn from the state and community, to not be in public life, to be out of office, retired, personal. For the ancient Roman, privacy had the sense of losing both the burdens and the honors of civic life, of retreating to the inner folds of one's own isolation. It may be a quiet and peaceful condition, but there is nothing noble, praiseworthy, or honorable about it. That there might be something disreputable or even shameful about what we keep from the public, consider the euphemisms derived from the Latin: *privates*, the genitals that have no business going public, and *privy*, an outhouse. Now, while none of this directly suggests transgression, it does point to a suspicion, lurking in the trails of language itself, that what goes on in private may run counter to the public good and the common interest. Might privacy then have its roots in our injustice, or in something like our sinfulness? Is privacy just a grudging accommodation to human imperfection, both the imperfection of the private person and the imperfection of those who would peer into his heart?

Consider the story of Noah and his vineyard. The naked human body can be a symbol of innocence. But far more often, it is a symbol, and more than a symbol—the reality—not only of our vulnerability but also of our aggression—*naked* aggression! Naked, we are exposed to the external forces of nature and, even more terribly, other human beings; as we have seen, having a body, *being* embodied, is what makes us vulnerable to torture. Our own bodies may be turned against us. Naked, we are also exposed to the internal forces of our own natures. One of the most important turning points in the Bible is when Adam and Eve, in the first moment after they lose their innocence, cover themselves up. That symbolic act points to a recognition of the injustice or vice latent in the human body, particularly in human sexuality. It is not that sex is evil, rather it is that our bodies separate us from one another; we recognize that our naked needs and desires, grounded in the body, can and often do set us apart and set us against one another. In the body's naked individuation lie the seeds of the injustice that can divide us. It is surely no accident that, as Saint Augustine noticed,[9] the sexual act is one that humans generally do in private. Although it can cement a union, it also marks an exclusion and a separation: a good that cannot be shared. Sexuality also marks the shame of the body: not because sex itself must be shameful, but because it is where we most radically experience that tyranny of our own body and its desires over us. Surely this is why Noah felt such rage against his son: for prying into the exposed secrets of his weakness, a weakness that might completely undermine the respect that he required as a leader and a public person.

Here we glimpse what links torture and privacy: in each case there is an attempt to break through the barrier that shields us from the gaze of others, to get at facts about us or knowledge we are not ready to display—or at least not to everyone, or maybe just not to the public authorities. And so we tend to think it a violation if someone reads our letters or diary, listens in to our conversations, bugs our phone, rummages through our trash, feigns friendship to learn secrets, photographs us unawares, spies through our windows, or enters our home uninvited. But the torturer too violates boundaries in order to get at the truth his victim wants to conceal.

We should not too easily condemn what may move the torturer and the eavesdropper—especially when they are official representatives of the community. There are bad people who would injure, kill, and steal from ordinary citizens, from citizens who by habit and disposition respect the rights of their fellows and make their contribution to the common good. There are those who would attack, undermine, seek to destroy the very basis of our common life together. These bad people do not spring up all of a sudden; we cannot wait to defend ourselves and others from them only at the moment of attack. They plot in secret. They prepare their attack, sometimes with great cunning. They seek to recruit others to their cause. Their project may be long delayed and carefully concealed. We can defend ourselves and each other from them only if we can learn about their intentions and preparations in plenty of time.[10] And since they will not give us that information willingly, we must get it from them—violently or by stealth, by torture or eavesdropping. And even after the deed has been done, the attack launched and defeated, the boundary of the person impedes our ability to do perfect justice: to punish the guilty, but only the guilty.

Our existence together as social beings is imperfect. In the tension between public and private, we face an epistemological problem in justice: we cannot always *know* what people have done, and even less can we know what they *intend* to do. We cannot get past the border of their skins. This is the foundational, epistemological gap in justice: human justice itself is deprived of perfect knowledge. If only we could see through to our fellows' hearts, if only we knew all that they do, then there would be no mistakes. The innocent would be rewarded, or at least left alone, and the guilty would meet justice. This inherent privacy of the human mind, and of the facts themselves, is what lures us to torture: to find a way to force a person to expose himself in all the nakedness of what he truly has done and plans to do. This wish, to know the minds of the unrighteous, is what we have so often understood as a feature of the divine wisdom and omniscience of the gods or God. From them nothing is hidden. They have no need to torture to get at the truth.

We do not possess the divine insight of true knowledge into deed and motive, yet the human community requires justice and this pushes us to do all we can to approximate complete understanding of people's acts and character. Those responsible for public order understandably resent impediments to their ferreting out and preventing crime if possible, punishing it if necessary. As long as there have been public officers, they have sought to bridge the epistemological gap between private intention, hidden guilt, and public knowledge for the sake of preventing and punishing crime in the name of the common good. In ancient Greece and Rome, slaves were thought to lack the honor to give truthful testimony, and so if their testimony was needed, it could only be produced under torture. In medieval law the reluctance to impose the death penalty unless guilt was absolutely certain led to doubts about eyewitness testimony and circumstantial evidence; only a confession would do. And so the recalcitrant would be tortured until he gave up the confession that would doom him—but only if proof that today would be thought sufficient pointed in his direction.[11]

And so in other times any approach—including torture and certainly eavesdropping—was available to those with legitimate investigative authority. Indeed, once the wall of privacy was breached, public officers saw no reason to ignore what might be called private vice and malign imaginings. Treason in England was originally defined as "compass[ing]" or "imagin[ing]" the death of the king.[12] So the state empowered its officers to sniff out not only who has done injustice but also who is *likely* to do injustice—and even who may want to subtract himself and all his inner and material resources from full and faithful service to the common good.

As we have noted, the concept of privacy has been used in a variety of ways and to cover all kinds of intrusions on our autonomy. We insist on the more central and familiar usage which would apply to our practical concern, the government's thirst for knowledge about us—whether it is slaked by violence or by stealth. Even in this core usage there are two strands to many, perhaps most privacy claims: one is the concern about how the private information will be used in order to threaten other interests, and the second is what might be called the pure privacy interest—that is, the interest in controlling information about oneself, quite apart from the threatening uses that might be made of it.

Take the first strand, the one implicated when governments— or neighbors—want to ferret out information in order to protect against secret plots and intentions. When people object to government collecting and analyzing information about us— whether it be Gerd Wiesler in the attic, or the NSA computers scanning cyberspace, or Department of Defense computers collating vast stores of public information to arrive at detailed patterns of our preferences, behaviors, and associations—they fear this information will be used to harass them with prosecutions, tax audits, denial of benefits, job loss.

In every such case, if the government's action is not justified, then *that* is the real grounds for complaint and that is where redress lies. But if the action is justified, then what complaint can we have that government learned facts—bridged the epistemological gap between inside and outside—that led it to take proper action? Critics of the government are the most frequent complainers about what they call violations of their privacy. But if the law protects against prosecution, harassment, job or benefits loss when a person criticizes government and opposes its policies, then that protection would seem to do everything anyone is entitled to. Yet if govern-ment snooping uncovers crime, fraud, or a disposition in an employee to disloyal acts, well surely that's good, not bad. To deny government the information that would lead it to pro-tect the community against dangerous, thieving, disloyal, or unreliable persons hardly seems a compelling purpose.

Privacy advocates sneer at this logic: it is a rationale that presupposes a benevolent government, a vigilant court system, and vigorous citizens ready and able to protect their rights against overreaching officials. But government, unlike the God of perfect justice, is often *not* benevolent, often paranoid, and sometimes just plain stupid; resistance to official malevo-lence, stupidity, or corruption can be expensive, cumbersome, and uncertain, so the surest way to avoid an entanglement with government that one is not sure to win is not to come into its sights at all. At its extreme, this view of privacy shields us from any inspection by the community and compels authority to catch any lawbreaking or aggression "in the act," without any recourse to the malefactor's own words or thoughts. There is a trace of this notion in the privilege against self-incrimination, by which a person cannot be forced to testify against—that is reveal—himself. But this privilege, enshrined in the Fifth Amendment,[13] has never been extended to self-revelations overheard or carelessly emitted without any official threat of pain or penalty.[14]

There is a fear here that cuts two ways: a fear of persons and a fear of governments. We have good reason to believe that others might do us injustice, not just because we have had the experience of others harming us, but, even more convincingly, because we recognize in ourselves the recurrent even if repressed urge to do harm ourselves. Despite the lure of injustice, or more properly because of it, we don't want injustice done to us. And even if we might not want to do it ourselves, we still know that we are capable of it, and that some goods that we desire shut others out. At the same time, we also know that in our embodied vulnerability, we need one another. "The human being is by nature the political animal," Aristotle wrote, and he meant precisely this: that we cannot live, much less live well, without one another in a political community. And politics demands justice, the ongoing public—not private—conversation and legislation concerning right and wrong, mine and thine.

So there is our dilemma. We have all done things, said things, certainly thought things that taken out of context, or even in context, might be interpreted as signs of a crime or of the intention to commit a crime. We all own things that might testify against us. A book, a letter, a souvenir, or some casual artifact might cast our associations, our thinking, our motives in a dark light. Pry deep enough, and there will be in all of our personal histories something that could tie us to a crime, whether rightly or wrongly. Before God, we could have confidence that these mute witnesses would be interpreted correctly. But before human investigators and judges? Once investigators begin, especially if given complete access to our lives, they have a terrible propensity to arrange and interpret the minute details of a life in a way that fits the crime, since it is in the nature of investigators to begin with the assumption that there has been or will be a crime. There is no way to approximate perfect knowledge; either you have it or you don't. And we don't. To act as if we did is not to approximate the divine; it is to parody it.

Privacy has its roots in this dilemma, in our inadequacy and our finitude. We are liable to be unjust, and so to be investigated. But our powers of knowledge and interpretation are limited, and so we may misconstrue what we find. To grant human investigators the powers of the divine is to give them a warrant that necessarily exceeds their abilities and will be misused and abused. The right of privacy is, admittedly, a second best, an acknowledgment of human imperfection. But it serves as a hedge against the worst excesses of that imperfection when it is married to political authority, even legitimate authority. Human beings should never stand absolutely naked before human authority—not literally as in Golub's painting, not metaphorically as in the Stasi captain listening in the apartment house attic, in all of our attics.

There is a second strand to the argument for privacy. It does not emphasize the concrete disadvantages that government may impose on us. It emphasizes rather the value of privacy to our sense of personal integrity before government and all others. This second strand fears no concrete disadvantage deriving from privacy invasions by individuals or the government.[15] Indeed, it lays claim to being the essence of privacy. By controlling information about yourself, you control who you are and who you can become. Think back to your adolescence and young adulthood. If there had been a permanent record easily available to all of everything you did and said (and wore), would you have been as free to become the person you are today? Facebook and personal blogs are ways in which the young, imagining an infinite present, mortgage their future to their immediate impulses, leaving permanent traces of what they will later wish quite literally to efface. And even as fully formed adults we might choose to present one face to our friends, another to our workplace collaborators, and still a third to the strangers we pass as we walk along the streets, shop, or sit in a restaurant. Indeed, there is still another presentation, the person we present to ourselves in all these encounters.

Here privacy is protecting our liberty to be whomever we wish to be: we become the person we present to the outside world, and this choice—really creation—of a persona is perhaps the deepest liberty of all, for through it, we maintain authority over who we *are* and *will be*. It allows us to be the authors of ourselves. In Max Beerbohm's *Happy Hypocrite: A Fairy Tale for Tired Men*,[16] the main character, wooing a woman of innocence and virtue, dons a mask to hide his face, which would otherwise reveal his immoral past. He then lives a life as virtuous as the face he portrays to the world. When he eventually must remove his mask, his true face has become as flawless as the mask he has been wearing. Once again, pervasive surveillance of our every move—as in George Orwell's *1984*—strips us of our humanity, just as the torturer strips (literally or figuratively) his victim of her humanity in the personal decomposition caused by great pain.

That said, this same liberty is bound up in a liberty to

deceive, defraud, and destroy others in the course of personal relations.[17] Joseph Conrad's Lord Jim flees the world that retains the memory of a youthful act of cowardice and dereliction—he along with several other officers abandoned a passenger ship they thought was in imminent danger of sinking, leaving eight hundred hapless pilgrims in the middle of the Indian Ocean—and becomes a genuine hero in a remote Malaysian village. Jim seeks privacy to escape his former self to become a new and better person. (Many countries seal the records of juvenile wrongdoing in order to grant the same liberty of self-refashioning.) At the end of the story, tragically, Jim once again fails those who trusted him—whether through misjudgment, cowardice, or cowardice masquerading as generosity to a vicious enemy.

And finally a civilized society protects the deepest intimacies of private life, because the very opportunity to share those with a chosen few is itself a gift that we would be unable to make to friends and lovers if everything were open and public. In this sense, privacy and intimacy are reciprocal.[18] And yet this same "liberty" may be the screen behind which hide seducers, bigamists, grifters, disloyal employees, traitors, and spies. Piercing privacy is how we protect ourselves against all kinds of deceptions and disappointments. A world in which everyone at all times were taken at face value would be dangerous to the point of unintelligibility, and perhaps uninteresting to the point of inanity. Ordinary citizens have an interest in piercing each others' privacy in a way analogous to the interest of government in piercing privacy to ferret out wrongdoers and protect the public. And in our personal lives, we have an interest in venturing into each other's privacy, in the subtle games of companionship, friendship, and love, to test the limits of trust, knowledge, and affinity.

So privacy is undoubtedly an important value, and the Stasi state of Captain Wiesler is monstrous in its denial. But it is not like torture. Torture is intrinsically evil; privacy both shields against evil and shields evil, it is constructive and destructive. Torture is absolutely wrong. Nothing like that can be said about violations of privacy. After all, the constitution forbids only *unreasonable* searches and seizures. And wiretaps, electronic snooping, and searches of papers and homes are all permissible with a warrant.[19] But most important is the obvious fact that however deeply felt the value of privacy may be in general, the boundaries and landmarks of privacy are largely conventional. What counts as the occasions and limits of intimacy, what information is thought of as confidential, and what intrusions and revelations are thought to violate privacy vary widely with the era, the nation, and the social milieu.[20]

The constitutional right to privacy is set out in the Fourth Amendment:

The right of the people to be secure in their persons, houses, papers, and effects, against unreasonable searches and seizures, shall not be violated, and no Warrants shall issue, but upon probable cause,

supported by Oath or affirmation, and particularly
describing the place to be searched, and the persons
or things to be seized.

As an eighteenth-century text, the amendment addressed
eighteenth-century controversies and abuses. Officers of government could not arbitrarily enter homes to search them
for contraband or evidence of crime. Nor could they arbitrarily seize property or arrest persons. These impositions
needed justification. They had to be reasonable or be supported by a warrant—which was a judicial order issued on
sworn evidence. Like several of the guarantees of the Bill of
Rights, addressed though it was to the issues of its time, the
Fourth Amendment stated a broader principle which has been
extrapolated from it and applied in different times to different circumstances, circumstances not imagined by those who
wrote or adopted those texts. Just as the First Amendment's
guarantee of the freedom of speech and the press has been
extrapolated to cover radio and television, so it has been necessary to decide whether wiretapping and electronic eavesdropping are searches. In 2001, in *Kyllo v. United States*[21] the
Supreme Court had to decide whether the use of a thermal
imaging device to detect the amounts and location of heat
coming from a house—the police suspected Kyllo was using
high-intensity lamps to grow marijuana—amounted to a
search of that home. Justice Antonin Scalia put the question
this way: "What are the limits on th[e] power of technology
to shrink the realm of guaranteed privacy"? And in reach-
ing the conclusion that this use of technology passed those

limits, Justice Scalia mused that such a device might even disclose "at what hour each night the lady of the house takes her daily sauna and bath."[22] And no doubt in our culture, or some segments of it, bathing would count as a private, indeed an intimate detail. In other contexts and to other sensibilities, that information would be far less private than when "the lady of the house" ate breakfast—sensibilities and cultures where bathing is a routinely public act, but eating where one could be seen is shameful.

The path for extrapolating from an eighteenth-century text and eighteenth-century sensibilities was traced by the Supreme Court's decision in the 1967 case *Katz v. United States.*[23] The Court treated as a violation of the Fourth Amendment the government's recording of a bookie's telephone calls by a device placed on the outside of a public telephone booth. The decision nicely illustrates the variable and elusive nature of the judgments on this topic. Justice John Marshall Harlan's concurring opinion best explains what the Court was deciding:

[T]he Fourth Amendment protects people, not places." The question, however, is what protection it affords to those people. . . . [T]here is a twofold requirement, first that a person have exhibited an actual (subjective) expectation of privacy and, second, that the expectation be one that society is prepared to recognize as "reasonable." Thus a man's home is, for most purposes, a place where he expects privacy, but . . . conversations in the open would not be protected against being overheard, for the expectation of privacy under the circumstances would be unreasonable.

The critical fact in this case is that "one who occupies it [a telephone booth], shuts the door behind him, and pays the toll that permits him to place a call is surely entitled to assume" that his conversation is not being intercepted.[24]

The key is the "reasonable expectation" of privacy, an expectation that is objectively reasonable. It is not just a subjective expectation, which is what you might have when confiding a secret to a faithless friend or in too loud a voice in a public place; the Court has told us that that is not protected. But if the law decrees, for instance, that telephone conversations or bank accounts are open to all, is an expectation that they are private any longer reasonable? Even if somewhat heroically we are prepared to say that a sufficiently widely shared social norm cannot constitutionally be immediately overridden by legislation, there must be a time and means for altering these norms. The objective or "reasonable expectation" standard for judging social intrusions on what we would subjectively like to keep private will depend, after all, on what society chooses to protect.[25]

Accordingly, though an intrinsic value, privacy cannot sensibly be declared an absolute value. It is not just that the boundary walls of privacy are inescapably conventional, but even within those boundaries, given enough urgency, the wall may be breached, broken down. Murder in the home is still murder. Here is another contrast between eavesdropping and torture. There must come a point where we have gone so far public that we have crossed the line of Harlan's criterion and as speakers (e-mailers, Web casters, bloggers) are no longer "entitled to assume that . . . conversation is not being intercepted." Whatever "expectation of privacy" we may have, it is no longer "reasonable."

Injustice hides itself. The common good requires that we find out who commits acts of injustice and why, so that injustice can be prevented or cured and the unjust punished. We know that the facts and the criminals do not willingly announce themselves, and so we must pry them out. But even beyond that and descending to the level of gossip and idle curiosity, sociability—the conditions of common life—entails (if it does not require) that we attain some, perhaps only minimal, level of familiarity with each other, that we take some interest in each other, even in the people we pass on the street or sit across from on the subway. A world without that would be so cold as to be brutal, inhuman. It is as if we owe each other some minimal level of self-revelation. So privacy is surely a value and an intrinsic one, but it is not even plausibly an absolute—unlike, as we have argued, the prohibition on torture.

The London Metropolitan Police force established its first plain-clothes detective division in 1842—the precursor of Scotland Yard—to serve as a "centralized, elite force to coordinate murder hunts."[26] This was a response to the great rise of awful crimes taking place in the increasingly anonymous world of modern industrial society. People recoiled at the idea of "detectives" eavesdropping on conversations or pawing through drawers and letters, even those of the lower classes. This was simply not something a gentleman, a lady, or a civilized society should allow. As Secretary of State Henry L. Stimson said in 1929, "Gentlemen do not read each other's mail." Yet Scotland Yard had been in operation for decades before Stimson spoke, and J. Edgar Hoover was hard at work at that very time, going on to found the FBI in 1935. There was no other way to develop modern law enforcement, given the new social dynamics: life was so urban and uprooted, law enforcement could not count on the close bonds and transparency typical of local, village life to get to the bottom of things.[27]

In this world of changing circumstances and expectations, eavesdropping is a very particular kind of invasion of privacy. It takes advantage of the medium of publicness that must obtain, in however limited a fashion, for two people (at the minimum) to communicate. When we choose to speak to someone, we make a decision to expose our internal thoughts, to bare them. The content might be trivial or momentous; it makes no difference. We have chosen to share something distinctly our own, our thoughts or feelings, with at least one other human being, and to do so we must make use of a public medium through which that sharing is possible. In doing so, we *intend* that medium to convey what is ours only to the person or persons targeted, but that does not mean that someone else might not take advantage of the essential publicness of the medium, at first, perhaps, to overhear by accident, but then to listen in, to eavesdrop, to steal what is essentially private.

What if we do not speak, but use sign language, or a letter, or an e-mail? In every case, the same thing is true: we are using a medium that allows the internal to come to external expression, to share what is ours with others. And others may take advantage of that public medium to spy on us.

The question is, can they ever do so *without* violating a right to privacy? If we say no, then it would never be permissible for anyone to testify in court to a conversation they happened to overhear. It would certainly never be right for police—with or without a warrant—to tap phones, read letters, or monitor e-mail. How then would we safeguard justice? How could we investigate suspects, monitor conspiracies, or demonstrate motivation? The prudential principle here is the Constitution's term "probable cause." This is not a hard-and-fast rule; it is governed by precedent and practical wisdom, but it might be the best we can do and it offers a well-grounded degree of protection against arbitrary abuse of investigative power.

As we have seen, the difficulty today is the challenge presented by developing technologies. In the nineteenth century when urban crime and urban anonymity had reached modern proportions, the chief of police in London might send an undercover detective to Victoria Station to prowl for suspects or clues in a specific case where there are very few leads. Should that officer disregard what he sees and hears? Is it an invasion of privacy—or perhaps a kind of profiling—for him to look at the way people dress, how they move, or what they carry, or to listen to the abrupt words they speak? In the days before sophisticated electronic surveillance, and because it was virtually impossible to introduce government agents into the Mafia, the FBI resorted to tactics such as parking on the street outside mob funerals and weddings and noting the license plate numbers of the cars the guests arrived in—an early version of data mining. Today Central London—and now parts of New York City—are blanketed with video cameras transmitting and recording everything that happens on the streets and in public places.[28] Should those who monitor the images disregard what they see? As with the nineteenth-century detective prowling in Victoria Station, we would say they should use their discretion to pick out only the details that are relevant to the danger at hand. Otherwise, there would be nowhere to start at all, and justice might miscarry before it even begins.

What do we do now, when a great deal of communication takes place, not by voice carried by sound waves, not by letter carried by the postal service, but in digital form through billions and billions of e-mails? Keep in mind that humans cannot possibly intercept and scrutinize every one of these: there would not be enough Gerd Wieslers in all the intelligence services and police forces in the country to sort through all of them. This must be done by electronic sorting mechanisms—machines do not blush—and the billions of communications winnowed down to a tiny fraction, which sentient beings may then read. Is not this sorting, this data mining, akin to the detective standing in Victoria Station, picking up trails of conversations and other clues?

Might we not say, then, that although what is considered

private varies greatly from time to time and place to place, at least this—for example, sexual intimacies—or that—for example, religious convictions—is always and everywhere protected as private? These very concrete suggestions are contradicted by wide and frequent experience. In the end the most one can confidently proclaim is that, whatever the details, law and society must leave the mind and person *some* substantial domain somewhere to which he may safely withdraw, free from unsought intrusions. This is quite different from the inviolability of the person in respect to her physical integrity, an inviolability that absolutely forbids torture and abuse.

Where we set the presumptive boundaries of privacy is to a great degree a matter of convention and historical practice. Political wisdom guides how we adjust these boundaries given changes in customs and technology, but the touchstone must always be a determination to balance the state's need to know with the state's inability to know perfectly and so its potential to do injustice. Thus, while we can confidently claim that privacy is intrinsically valuable, to claim that it is absolute makes no sense: its boundaries are set by custom and law, and every intrusion on privacy might in exigent circumstances be justified if only certain limits—themselves circumstantial—are observed. We as a people forbid only "unreasonable" searches and allow for search warrants. That seems sensible—but we would not grant the state power to engage in "reasonable" torture or, *pace* Professor Dershowitz, institute a system of torture warrants.

NO BEGINNING OR NO END

THE FOUNDERS OF the United States understood that politics necessarily involves risk, *personal* risk for those who engage in it, especially at the level of national leadership. President George W. Bush came into office in 2001 with no great sense of that risk. He had traveled outside of the country scarcely at all, and so his vision was fixed on his plan for lifting burdens from the people: reducing taxes, improving schools, reforming Social Security. The events of 9/11 yanked his focus away from pleasing the people to protecting them from a threat—perhaps a mortal threat—unlike any they had known. Instead of a risk no greater than the failure of an amiable domestic project, he suddenly faced great dangers: not only material danger and political danger, but also moral danger—moral danger for him, for his officers, and for the American people.

The signers of the Declaration of Independence understood the risks they were running, risks that political leaders in times of war and upheaval always run. They concluded their declaration with these words: "And for the support of this

Declaration, with a firm reliance on the protection of divine Providence, we mutually pledge to each other our Lives, our Fortunes and our sacred Honor." They were willing to risk everything: if they failed, their lives and property would be forfeited for their act of treason. But *honor* alone they designated as *sacred*, perhaps because risking so much, and defying an authority long revered, demanded that they act with seriousness of purpose for the sake of a common cause that is genuinely noble.

There is no reason to believe that President Bush too, in his response to 9/11, was moved by anything other than a similar sense of honor, the sense of an unexpected, awesome responsibility, and the imperative to do his duty. And his first response was to direct those around him to do whatever was necessary to protect the nation and its people from another attack. Like other presidents before him—Jefferson, Lincoln, Franklin Roosevelt, but especially Lincoln—he thought that the crisis he faced required him to break the law. He desperately needed knowledge, intelligence about the enemy that had struck the nation, and he was willing to take any action to get it. His program of harsh interrogation and ubiquitous electronic surveillance broke the law: our laws and treaty obligations against torture and the 1978 Foreign Intelligence Surveillance Act (FISA).

Whatever you might think about drawing a parallel between George Bush and Abraham Lincoln, the crisis each confronted was—if not the same—of a similar order of magnitude. Some have argued that terrorism, though horrible in specific cases, is really only a tactical nuisance, not a genuine threat to national survival, and therefore requires only a law-enforcement response. But a fair assessment of the threat reports the government received after 9/11, with credible intelligence that Al Qaeda was seeking to deliver chemical, biological, and radioactive weapons, shows that the Bush administration was not wrong to see itself confronted with a possible national calamity: tens of thousands of deaths, many more injuries, and disruption of social, political, and economic systems.[1] So dire was the threat that a national commission of senior nongovernmental experts was convened to formulate political structures to cope with the possibility of the death in one blow of large numbers of members of Congress.[2]

In the late spring and early summer of 1861, Lincoln found the United States in a precarious position. The southern states were in open rebellion, arsenals were being seized, hostile militias were forming, and the federal garrison at Fort Sumter had been bombarded. Washington, D.C., the seat of the federal government, its territory carved out of Maryland—a state boiling over with pro-slavery, secessionist sentiment—lay on the very border of Virginia, the leading state of the newborn Confederacy. Under the circumstances, Lincoln took it upon himself to raise an army and to intern rebel sympathizers, in each case without immediate congressional authorization as required by the Constitution. But Lincoln did not arrogate these powers to himself as a matter of course; instead, on July 4, he gave a special address to the two houses of Congress. He openly discussed what he had done, recognizing that he had acted against the letter of the Constitution and his oath as president to "take care that the laws be faithfully executed."

At the same time, Lincoln pointed out that all the laws of the nation were being resisted by the rebellious states, and that he must take responsibility for that too by actively working to end the rebellion, even if this meant violating some laws. He posed the problem to Congress as follows:

> To state the question more directly, are all the laws but one to go unexecuted and the Government itself go to pieces lest that one be violated? Even in such a case would not the official oath be broken if the Government should be overthrown, when it was believed that disregarding the single law would tend to preserve it? [3]

Lincoln's claim was that necessity might force him to break one law (taking it upon himself to suspend habeas corpus) to save the body of laws as a whole. Indeed Lincoln was quite muscular in his assertion of executive authority. When Chief Justice Roger B. Taney ordered that John Merryman, an accused saboteur held in Fort McHenry, be produced before him in Baltimore, the general in charge of the fort not only refused but barred entry to the fort by the United States marshal sent by Taney.[4] Lincoln had done his duty as he saw it; now Congress must do its duty and decide if he had acted rightly in an emergency. Recognizing the crisis that Lincoln faced, one that demanded urgent and efficient action, Congress ratified Lincoln's acts, allowing the raising of troops and the suspension of habeas corpus. Five years later, in 1866, after the war was over and Lincoln dead, the Supreme Court held in *Ex Parte Milligan* that not only was Lincoln wrong to suspend the writ—only Congress could do that—but Congress could not later make Lincoln's unlawful suspension right. As to the claim that the desperate urgency of the moment gave Lincoln the right to act, Justice Davis, writing for the Court, thundered that such a "pernicious" doctrine would lead "directly to anarchy or despotism."[5] Nevertheless, Justice Davis was also strikingly sympathetic to Lincoln's urgent need to act during the "late wicked rebellion," yet now that "public safety is assured," those illegally detained must be allowed redress for the wrong they had suffered, a wrong that Congress's ratification could not make right.

There were precedents for what Lincoln did in acting in an emergency before he could get Congress's assent. In 1807, the United States was still a very young nation, its Constitution only twenty years old. Great Britain, the former master and global power, considered its loss at Yorktown but a transient setback, and had chosen not to accept fully the independence of its former colonies. A sign of this attitude was that British warships claimed the prerogative to board American vessels and press into service any seaman deemed to be a British subject. Americans were increasingly angered and alarmed at violations of their nation's sovereignty and their citizens' rights. Then, in what was to become a famous diplomatic imbroglio, the British warship *Leopard* confronted the American frigate *Chesapeake* on June 22, 1807, and demanded permission to board in search of deserters.[6] When the captain of the *Chesapeake* refused, the *Leopard* attacked, crippling the *Chesapeake* and carrying off four crewmen, one of whom was later hanged for desertion.

The public reaction in America was swift and furious. Citizens in Norfolk, the home port of the *Chesapeake*, ran riot and destroyed British stores. Other ports declared their refusal to provide communications and supplies to British ships. From South to North, many called for revenge to uphold the nation's honor and independence in the face of this humiliation. Militias formed and patrolled the coast, shadowing the British warships. British communiqués seemed to threaten to blockade American ports in response to such hostile reactions. Fearing an imminent war, President Thomas Jefferson recognized how ill-prepared the newborn United States would be against the might of Great Britain. The United States had only the barest scraps of a navy, while the British had the most massive one on the globe, with sailors and marines well seasoned in the wars against Napoleon. And so Jefferson proceeded on his own authority to spend money to better equip and supply U.S. naval vessels against such hostile acts, even though the Constitution (Article I, section 9, clause 7) states, "No money shall be drawn from the Treasury, but in consequence of appropriations made by law." Writing in 1810, Jefferson explained in a private letter what he had done as president:

Ought the Executive, in that case, and with that foreknowledge, to have secured the good to his country, and to have trusted to their justice for the transgression of the law? I think he ought, and that the act would have been approved. After the affair of the Chesapeake, we thought war a very possible result. Our magazines were illy provided with some necessary articles, nor had any appropriations been made [by Congress] for their purchase. We [that is, Jefferson's administration] ventured, however, to provide them, and to place our country in safety; and stating the case to Congress, they sanctioned the act. [7]

Responding to a national sense of emergency, Congress did indeed ratify Jefferson's arguably unconstitutional acts after the fact, as it did Lincoln's some sixty years later.

Nearly two hundred years later, among the actions President Bush authorized in response to the 9/11 attacks were the arrest and detention of more than one thousand aliens from Islamic countries; the President's Surveillance Program, which included the interception of electronic messages to and from the United States where there was a suspicion that one of the parties to the communication belonged to a terrorist organization, as well as certain classified and undisclosed surveillance and intelligence-gathering measures; and means of interrogation according to an opinion procured from the Office of Legal Counsel defining torture in terms so narrow as to allow, among other things, waterboarding, sleep deprivation, shaking, wall-banging, slapping, and compelled maintenance of stressful and painful positions.[8]

The torture program was doubly problematic: In addition to violating U.S. laws and treaty obligations, it violated the dictates of humanity that we set out in earlier chapters. We do not have to brand President Bush as one of the "wicked men" that Justice Davis warned of, in order to take note of his radical departure from the behavior of Jefferson and Lincoln in a time of crisis. The latter two both openly recognized the danger in their own actions, and acknowledged that they had violated the Constitution, seeking ratification by Congress after the fact. Bush and his administration insisted that the power of the president to violate the law was an entailment of presidential authority to act in his capacity as commander in chief in a time of war and emergency, allowing Congress only so much oversight as he could not avoid or evade. At issue is not any one president, but rather, as Justice Davis wrote, "dangers to human liberty [that] are frightful to contemplate."

SURVEILLANCE AND ILLEGALITY

The President's Surveillance Program was problematic because it did not comply with FISA, which required authorization from the special Foreign Intelligence Surveillance Court (FISC) for electronic surveillance. FISA did allow some narrow emergency exceptions to the requirement of FISC authorizations, but only if "for a period not to exceed fifteen calendar days following a declaration of war by the Congress, and only if promptly reported to the Court and Congress."[9] The White House argued publicly and privately to congressional leaders that the growth, diffusion, and diversification of means of electronic communications since 1978 made many of FISA's provisions obsolete, as did the nature of the terrorist threat, which was based in no territory and tied to no government.

The requirement of a warrant was inapposite to techniques that allowed electronic scanning, with no human intervention, of literally billions of pieces of information in cyberspace (on Web sites, in e-mails and telephone messages), in order to detect patterns pointing to individuals and sites, and then only after further electronic winnowing to identify suspect persons or sources with sufficient precision to satisfy a FISA warrant. But the initial scanning activities would themselves seem to require a demonstration to FISC that there was probable cause or even only reasonable suspicion that each and every intercepted communication concerned potential hostile activity.[10] Such a demonstration at that preliminary stage could not possibly be made. (Because so much of the Surveillance Program remains classified—understandably so: its revelation would make it ineffective—it is not possible to do more than guess at its features and the ways in which it violated the statute.)

In a sense, the administration could have claimed that 9/11 left the United States exposed just as the outbreak of civil war had left Washington in 1861, although now in an entirely new technological context, and that therefore emergency action must be taken. The principal justifications for the apparent violations of FISA offered by the president and his lawyers were the obsolete nature of the 1978 FISA restrictions and the claim that the president's "inherent" powers as commander in chief during wartime could not constitutionally be constrained by Congress in the way FISA (or the statutory prohibition of torture) purported to do.[11] (Few doubted that the 2001 Congressional Authorization for the Use of Military Force was the equivalent of a declaration of a state of war. The

Korean and first Gulf wars had proceeded on such authorizations.) Both justifications might be gathered under the name "executive prerogative." The differences between Jefferson's and Lincoln's invocation of executive prerogative and Bush's are crucial.

EXECUTIVE PRIVILEGE AND THE
LIMITS OF LAW

The modern name we give to rulers, *the executive*, implies someone who takes action and follows through according to the directives of a higher authority. Just what is it that the executive *executes*? Our ordinary answer would be the law. We tend to distinguish law-making and executive functions of government, and we usually hold that the executive, as well as anyone entrusted with duties as a public servant, is bound by the law and that lawmaking is bound in turn by the legislators' responsibility to advance the common good.

The first justification for ignoring or going beyond the law harks back to an argument first made by Aristotle about the inevitably incomplete and approximate nature of laws. The second invokes the argument for executive prerogative not only set out by John Locke in the seventeenth century, a prophet of the American Revolution and of our conception of our republic, but also elaborated in a variety of ways—most menacingly by the twentieth-century German political theorist Carl Schmitt, some of whose arguments are eerily similar to those of the Bush Justice Department in its claims for the virtually unlimited powers of the president as commander in chief in times of crisis. Vice President Dick Cheney and his counsel, David Addington, procured from the Office of Legal Counsel an opinion by which the president would never run the risk of violating the law because in his role as commander in chief, Schmitt-like, his dictates are the law:

> [T]he Department of Justice could not enforce Section 2340A [U.S. law prohibiting torture] against federal officials acting pursuant to the President's constitutional authority to wage a military campaign. . . . Within the limits that the Constitution itself imposes, the scope and distribution of the powers to protect national security must be construed to authorize the most efficacious defense of the nation and its interest in accordance "with the realistic purposes of the entire instrument."[12]

We are reminded of Supreme Court Justice Robert Jackson's observation in 1952: "The Constitution did not contemplate that the title Commander-in-Chief of the Army and Navy will constitute him also Commander-in-Chief of the country."[13]

Let us begin with the ancient, Aristotle, for he is closer to us than you might expect. But first, some stories.

In a recent book about how judges interpret the law, Supreme Court Justice Stephen Breyer tells of a French teacher returning to Paris by train from holiday with a basket of two-dozen live snails to show his biology class. The railway's rule book prescribed that "travelers cannot bring animals on the train unless they are carried in a basket," and "if the traveler carries an animal in a basket, the traveler must pay half-fare for the animal." The conductor demanded that the teacher buy a half-fare ticket for the snails, despite the teacher's protest that surely the rule did not refer to snails.[14]

For Justice Breyer, this case is particularly delicious because it illustrates so vividly the kind of difficulty a judge must regularly face in making sense of the law and its intent. Did the framers of the statute envision that an "animal" would include snails? Didn't they mean only animals that would take up space or possibly cause a disturbance, such as dogs, cats, or maybe an occasional goat or chicken? We feel the absurdity of the case, for after all, as Justice Breyer wryly observes, if the conductor had to insist on treating the snails as animals by the letter of the law, why not then require twenty-four half-fare tickets for the two-dozen gastropods? Or is the ticket only for the basket, and not its number of occupants?

But a judge—as Justice Davis acknowledged—enjoys a certain luxury: he decides these questions at a distance, after those involved have taken action based on their understanding of the law at the time. The basket of snails might illustrate a key issue in the theory of legal interpretation, but what we consider here is the predicament of the person who must act, in the heat of the moment and under pressure of emergency. The conductor, as petty as the case might be, is an officer with a responsibility to execute the law, or at least to enforce a rule. Does any such officer, entrusted with a duty, have the right to substitute his own judgment for the rule if, in an unexpected case, an otherwise sensible rule turns out to be absurd?

And what if what is at stake is not something petty, like a basket of snails, but rather something of tremendous value, such as a human life?

In the middle of St. Peter's Square in the Vatican stands an imposing obelisk set there in 1586 as one of the most astonishing public works accomplished by Pope Sixtus V. Brought to Rome by the Emperor Caligula as plunder from the Temple of the Sun in Heliopolis, Egypt, it stands at eighty-six feet tall and weighs 331 tons. The architect Domenico Fontana won a competition from among hundreds of contenders for his plan to move and erect this immense object. His plan involved encasing the obelisk in an elaborate wooden frame and rolling it across logs to the square, all of which took over a year, employing hundreds of animals and human laborers. To set the object upright on its base, Fontana had designed an even larger crane-like mechanism. On September 14, the Feast of the Exaltation of the Cross, a huge crowd, many from far beyond Rome, gathered to watch this engineering marvel.

Pope Sixtus took extraordinary precautions. Because erecting the obelisk with Fontana's gigantic crane would be a delicate and precarious operation, and because of the potentially unruly crowd, Sixtus decreed that there be absolute silence on the site, on pain of death, so that the commanding engineers could shout their orders to the hundreds of workmen and be heard. Sixtus even had a gallows built on the spot to show he meant his order seriously. A tale, perhaps apocryphal but often repeated, has it that as the obelisk was rising, an astute sailor, who saw the ropes on the winches fraying and smoking under the immense friction, shouted out, *"Acqua alle corde!"*—Wet the ropes! His advice was heeded, the obelisk was saved and rose into position, and so it stands to this day. The grateful Pope thanked the sailor and awarded his family the right to send palms to St. Peter's for the celebration of Palm Sunday.[15]

True or not, this tale gets to the heart of something we naturally feel to be true: in an emergency, the letter of the law is not as important as its intent, and that intent may itself be nowhere expressed in the actual written law. In the story of the obelisk, the sailor is not even an officer of the Pope, but he nevertheless takes the full responsibility of the situation upon himself, at risk to his own life. How could the Pope do anything but pardon and even reward the sailor, despite his literal disobedience? Would we really want to say that the Pope had failed in his responsibility to the law he had made?

The sailor of the story is a private citizen, but we might say that officers of the law, and especially the chief executive of the state, have a special responsibility to apply the law equally in all cases and to show that they do not hold themselves and their own judgment above the law, even and especially in an emergency. Political theorists tend to discuss such emergencies in the abstract or in highly dramatic, potentially catastrophic scenarios, which has the effect of quarantining what is at stake to the distant realms of myth and high politics. Perhaps the following scenario might be instructive for how the matter might affect any one of us:

You are in a playground with a child in your care. The child suddenly and unexpectedly has an accident with potentially deadly consequences: a seizure, a deep cut, or perhaps a severe allergic reaction to a bee sting—whatever you would most vividly imagine as a emergency. Assume, too, that there is not enough time to wait for an ambulance. All you have is your car, and you know where a nearby hospital is. So you manage to carry the child to the car and start driving. You keep your cool as best you can, but in your haste, you sideswipe other cars and violate several traffic laws, some quite serious, such as speeding through a school zone and stoplights. Officers in a police cruiser spot you doing this, give chase, and pull you over. You show them the child, who is in obvious and acute distress. What should the officers do? You have clearly broken many laws, and as executives of the law, with a duty to enforce it, they should arrest you. But if they do, the child may die. So should they let you go? Give you an escort? Leave you and take the child themselves?

When this dilemma was presented at a public talk, a police officer in the audience gave a three-word answer: "Serve and protect." For him, that would mean ignoring the statute law in this case and getting the injured child to the hospital as fast and as safely as possible. In fact, situations such as this crop up all the time in law enforcement. On the afternoon of November 18, 2008, in a suburb of Boston, Jennifer Davis went into labor. Her husband, John, struggled to drive her to the hospital through rush-hour traffic. Two state troopers waived them through onto the breakdown lane so that they could make progress, but at another point in traffic, a third trooper stopped them and wrote them a ticket, even as they tried to explain the emergency. As a Massachusetts State

Police spokesman said, "The trooper made a judgment call to enforce the law governing the use of the breakdown lane."[16]

The philosopher Aristotle would have recognized each of these cases (even that of the basket of snails) as instances at the limit of law, a domain that requires the special virtue that he called *epieikeia*. We could translate this as "equity," "decency," or "reasonableness." For Aristotle, it would be a form of injustice for the officers to be sticklers for the law: halting you and putting an injured child or pregnant woman at serious risk; it would be *reasonable* for them to use their own judgment for how best to "serve and protect." After all, "serve and protect" would be an entirely recognizable motto for Aristotle's view that what makes a government legitimate is that it advances the common good. Aristotle put the key point this way:

> The cause of this problem is that all law is general, but in some cases, it is not correct to dictate according to . . . a general rule. And this really is the essential nature of the reasonable: the rectification of the law when it is defective because of its generality.[17]

"The reasonable" (*epieikeia*) indicates a form of justice that comes into play when a rule fails to accomplish its intended purpose *in a particular case*. It is the *nature* of human action that its complexity cannot be adequately captured in advance by general rules. Aristotle argued that every area of study has a degree of precision appropriate to it.[18] In physics and mathematics, we expect the highest standards of rigor for how the rules conform to action and the so-called real world. But ethics, justice, and law are another matter. We cannot expect the same rigor, and this is because the terms themselves, the contexts, contingencies, and complications of human action, are so unpredictable that it is impossible to completely circumscribe them with universal rules.

This does not mean that we should not have rules at all, only that we should understand the limits of these rules. When a lawmaker—be it an individual monarch or a popular assembly—sets down a law, that legislator is making a *general* rule that will necessarily fail to foresee every possible circumstance. A law, in effect, makes a judgment about circumstances in the future and tells us what we must do, under the threat of force or sanction, without consulting the particulars. It cannot take these details into account because when the law is passed, these events have not happened, and no lawmaker can anticipate every contingency. Law, then, decides and commands in advance of the specifics. But no general rule, applied in advance of the actual circumstances, can always get things right.

So why have rules and laws at all? Why not allow the ruler, public servants, police officers, railway conductors, or even private citizens like the sailor to decide each case as it arises? Because the result will tend either to anarchy or to tyranny. For the most part, the weakness we have just identified in the law is usually its strength. Law, by its nature, dictates *katholou*: generally, universally. It makes a judgment prior to any particular case. And for Aristotle, this is what we seek, at least in part, in the rule of law. Ruling generally, law attempts to take human weakness out of the equation by preventing personal considerations from swaying judgment in a particular case. "This is why we do not permit a human being to rule, but rather law, because the human being acts in his own interest and becomes a tyrant."[19] Judgment according to personal preference is the essence of the tyrant's arbitrary power. That law is universal and generally insensitive to private wishes is usually one of its greatest virtues.

Here we have it: our sense that the rule of law, not of human beings, is fundamental to our freedom. In Robert Bolt's *A Man for All Seasons*, Thomas More challenges his son-in-law, William Roper, who would violate every law of the land, to lay hold of the Devil: "This country is planted thick with laws, from coast to coast, Man's laws, not God's! And if you cut them down, and you're just the man to do it, do you really think you could stand upright in the winds that would blow then?"[20] The law is our defense against tyranny, the arbitrary imposition of one person's will over all others, and against anarchy, the ungoverned combat of many people's wills. If we cut down the laws to lay hold of our enemies, where do we hide when the Devil turns round on us, armed with the power of the state? The "Dirty Harry" (or Dirty Roper) fantasy naively assumes that the righteous and the good will be the ones wielding power. But if the good wield power to shortcut the law, even for a noble purpose, then the authority of the ruler becomes even more of a prize for those who would grab it for tyrannical ends of their own, and so they will slowly but fatally insinuate themselves into the paths of that expanded power to rise to positions where they can do just that.

But the rule of law, and not of human beings, presents the problem of the exceptional case: the law is a substitute for human judgment in each particular case on its individual merits. And sometimes what the law commands blindly goes against what any reasonable person would require. So, in the examples of police officers and traffic violations, it misses the point to say, "But why can't we just have a law that allows police officers to overlook such violations and offer escorts in cases of emergency?" No matter how many exceptions are written into law in an attempt to cover the quirkiness of reality, there will always be another unanticipated context in which it would be better for all involved to ignore or break some law, at least in that one circumstance. There will always be some other unexpected convergence of events that the lawmaker did not predict. Law can never be made perfectly whole, and no amount of fine-tuning will ever make it so.

Nor can we square this circle by writing into the law a general provision like the Model Penal Code's defense of necessity:

> (1) Conduct which the actor believes to be necessary to avoid an evil to himself or another is justifiable, provided that: (a) the evil sought to be avoided by such conduct is greater than that sought to be prevented by the law defining the offense charged.[21]

Such a provision either is too broad, inviting a weighing of advantages in every case by everyone subject to it—citizens and officers—and thus giving up the very value of law, which is its generality (the rule of law becomes no more than a rule of thumb), or is limited to specific instances, persons, and measures—and then the need to recognize unexpected exceptions pops up again.

Aristotle's treatment goes strongly against our modern legalist sensibilities. The inability of law to achieve justice in all cases leads Aristotle to prefer monarchy, at least in principle: "Whenever it happens, then, that there is a whole family, or even some one individual among the rest, whose virtue is so superior as to exceed that of all the others, it is just for this family to be the kingly family and to control everything, and for this one individual to be king."[22] Law is but a substitute for reason applied with practical wisdom in every given circumstance, and if there were a person of exceptional moral virtue to heed the common good and of intellectual virtue to grasp how to cultivate that good at every important juncture, that person, and not the law, should rule. Law alone, though instituted by reason, is reason made mindless—in the sense that it forecloses deliberation about what would be best in this place, at this time, in this configuration of people and events.

Imagine you are on a flight crossing the Pacific Ocean. For some reason, the pilots become disabled—the result of a sudden illness, an accident, or an attack, it does not matter. Who should now pilot the airplane? A passenger chosen by lot? A representative committee of passengers? The richest person in first class? But if there were, by chance, an off-duty pilot traveling as a passenger, wouldn't you want him or her to fly the plane? Wouldn't that be the obvious solution?

Or consider the same trans-Pacific flight, only this time

a passenger goes into shock due to a severe allergy attack. Without immediate assistance, she will die from asphyxiation, and you are hours from an airport. Again, if there were a doctor or nurse on board, wouldn't the obvious remedy be for the medical professional to perform an emergency tracheotomy, not for a flight attendant or random passengers to do whatever they happen to guess might work? If the nurse or doctor uses a plastic dinner knife rather than a scalpel, and a ballpoint pen casing rather than medical tubing, to complete the surgery, would you have any objection?

The first scenario, with the disabled pilots, is a version of the ancient ship-of-state metaphor for politics, one as old as Plato's *Republic*.[23] We are all "in the same boat." There is an obvious common good, our survival. Even a small error in piloting could result in all of our deaths. What we would all agree on, then, is that someone with expert knowledge in piloting should "rule" the "ship." We would not hesitate to turn the helm over to such a person. Think of the qualities exemplified by Captain Chesley Burnett Sullenberger III, who was able to land US Airways Flight 1549 in the Hudson River, after a flock of birds disabled its engines, without losing a single one of his 155 passengers: his success depended on an extraordinarily rare combination of not only skill and knowledge but also the moral character needed to remain calm and to lead in such a crisis.[24] The force of the metaphor, of course, is that politics is like piloting a ship or aircraft: both our lives and our *way* of life are at stake, and to secure them well demands an exceptional combination of skill, knowledge, and moral character. If we could find a person, or better still, a family that could produce such leaders over the generations, wouldn't we do better to turn rule over to them?

If the first scenario, the airplane without a pilot, illuminates *who* should rule on Aristotle's account, the second scenario, the emergency tracheotomy, also shows *how* that person should rule. In fact, Aristotle argued along just these lines:[25] We expect a doctor to know the standard medical practice for injuries and illnesses, but we also trust a truly fine physician to depart from the textbook procedures when conditions depart from the norm. Above all, we count on the physician to know when the norm no longer offers guidance in exceptional cases, and the master of medicine will still know what to do, or at least what to try, in such cases. No ordinary person will have that skill; it is a matter of specialized knowledge combined with a highly refined practical know-how that only very few can possess. The question then becomes whether we trust a political leader—Jefferson, Lincoln, or Bush—to have the analogous know-how to depart from the "textbook" standards of politics and law in a true emergency.

For Aristotle, then, the decisive question, following this analogy, is "whether it is more beneficial to be ruled by the best man or by the best laws."[26] Even the best laws, like the best medical procedures as laid down by the textbooks and hospital protocols, will sometimes fail to capture what specific circumstances require. Certainly it is good to have good, or even the best, rules, protocols, and laws; but because no system of rules can ever be adequate to deal with the complexity of reality, it is even better to have someone whose understanding and skill are so outstanding that he or she knows when and how to depart from these rules when it is truly necessary. This does not mean that Aristotle's model ruler simply abandons the rule of law and systems of statutes in favor of governance by fiat, no more than a great doctor would abandon general procedures, training, or protocol. His key to good practice in each case is the practical wisdom to know when and how to depart from the norm without destroying it.

If Aristotle himself recognized the threat of arbitrary power, of tyranny, in giving a human being precedence over the law, how much more was this present to the minds of the founders of our republic and to the thinkers, especially Locke and Montesquieu, who provided them with their intellectual, moral, and rhetorical groundwork: the rights of man, the separation of powers, the rule of law. Yet Locke, in the *Second Treatise on Government*, declares that "Salus Populi Suprema Lex [the welfare of the people is the supreme law], is certainly so just and fundamental a Rule, that he, who sincerely follows it, cannot dangerously err."[27] Locke gave the name *prerogative* to the "Power to act according to discretion, for the publick good without the prescription of the Law, and sometimes even against it."[28] Locke declares that "tis fit that the Laws themselves should in some Cases give way to the Executive Power, or rather to this Fundamental Law of Nature and Government, viz. That as much as may be, all the Members of the Society are to be preserved."[29]

Yet Locke remains deeply skeptical that any human being entrusted with the power to rule could possess in any sustained way the nearly divine wisdom necessary to act beyond the guidance and restraints of law. "[T]he Reigns of good

Princes have been always most dangerous to the Liberties of their People."[30] When a good and wise prince does something manifestly for the common good, even if against the law, that prerogative to act contrary to law risks becoming assumed as a royal right to do so arbitrarily. This is the great danger that Justice Davis spoke of in the *Milligan* case, and it is the question we must always pose when a president assumes extraordinary powers. In the end, the intentions and even the beneficial results of a good ruler acting outside of law are not as important as the precedent he sets, both for the respect for the rule of law and for the institutional role of the executive, and this is why reverence or disdain for Bush is entirely beside the point. A good ruler leaves a precedent for a corrupt successor, or even a well-meaning but inadequate one.[31] In fact, a good ruler leaves a dangerous precedent even for himself, because over time he may change and become biased, corrupt, or perhaps just debilitated or senile.

This is a decisive divide. Locke has no faith that, as Aristotle says, "a whole family, or even some one individual" will be so superior in wisdom that such authority to act beyond the law, not just in exceptional cases but in any case, will endure for long. Locke places his faith not in the virtue of rulers but in the virtue of institutions and, ultimately, in the consent of the people. Since Locke also accepts that the power of prerogative is a necessary one, he asks, "But who shall be Judge when this Power [of prerogative] is made a right use of?" His answer is that "there can be no Judge on Earth," but this does not mean passive acceptance of ill rule: "The People have no other remedy in this, as in all other cases where they have no Judge on Earth, but to appeal to Heaven" (section 168), which for Locke means the appeal to force of arms and the people's right of revolution.

We moderns are very suspicious of the idea that there can be rulers possessing an almost divine wisdom, and we are quite unwilling to admit that such wisdom can be passed on in a monarchical succession. We constrain the prince in the pursuit of our good because of his imperfect knowledge and our imperfect trust in him. Hence the rule of law and a government defined by checks and balances. This was never put better than by Supreme Court Justice Robert Jackson when in 1952 he rejected President Truman's assertion of implicit emergency power to seize the nation's steel mills to ensure defense production during the Korean War: "Such power either has no beginning or it has no end. If it exists, it need submit to no legal restraint. I am not alarmed that it would plunge us straightway into dictatorship, but it is at least a step in that wrong direction."[32]

And yet for all the eloquence of Jackson's phrase, surely it is Aristotle and Locke who spoke rightly and Jefferson and Lincoln who acted rightly. Whether Bush did is the question before us. In the same letter quoted earlier, Jefferson declares, "A strict observance of the written law is doubtless one of the high duties of a good citizen, but it is not the highest. . . . To lose our country by a scrupulous adherence to written law, would be to lose the law itself, with life, liberty, property and all those who are enjoying them with us."[33] And it is to Jefferson and Lincoln we must look when we judge what President Bush did in the first days and weeks after 9/11 when he authorized the President's Surveillance Program as well as the temporary detention of some thousand aliens from the same countries from which the attackers had come.

Recall the account in the previous chapter of how unavoidably conventional is the right to privacy. There may be a core to privacy that every law and custom must respect if there is to be privacy at all, but it is law and custom that trace the outlines of that right. Persons, homes, books, and papers are secure, in the words of the Constitution, only against "unreasonable searches and seizures"; almost any privacy can be violated with a warrant "upon probable cause." Thus not only are the boundaries of privacy in physical space conventional, so too are the conceptual boundaries of privacy: it is marked out by a kind of conventional or legal hyperspace. And if so, is it not fetishistic to invest those boundaries with the same kind of inviolability for which we have argued in describing the absolute wrong of torture? To put it in the constitutional terms of the Fourth Amendment, were not the measures of the President's Surveillance Program reasonable, the "seizures" of electronic information not unreasonable?

LEARNING NOT TO BE GOOD

WE ADMIT, ALONG with Lincoln and Jefferson, that the restraints of the rule of law must be loosened when law is unable to preserve us against an unexpected crisis. The real difficulty here is not the sadist in the case of torture nor the pathological snoop in the case of violations of privacy, but the duly authorized agents of the state who might legitimately seek otherwise hidden information in order to assure the safety of the community. We have argued that torture, as a way of gaining knowledge even in case of desperate need, is absolutely wrong. We have argued that the violation of privacy for similar ends, while always distasteful and ordinarily wrong, is not absolutely wrong in the way that torture is. No one but a monster would deny that in the context of our daily lives the infliction of terrible pain must seem so unthinkable and so clearly immoral that the very idea that we should need to make an argument against such a practice would appear absurd and repulsive. But can anything be *absolutely* wrong, in the face of the extreme circumstances faced by Jefferson, Lincoln, and Bush? At the heart of the matter is the distinction between private morality and political responsibility.[1]

The very fact that we are seriously discussing the use of torture at this time in our history, almost a decade after 9/11, shows that there is something more at stake, something that calls into question the adequacy of our everyday morality.

At stake is the very survival of the political community and the good that the political community can secure for its members. It is an ancient insight that, as Aristotle put it, the human being is a *zoôn politikon*, one whose very life is defined by the necessity of existing together with others in a political community in order for both individuals and the community as a whole to survive, and beyond that, to thrive, to achieve a life that is the best and most noble.[2] It is *within* the community that the absolute prohibition of torture and the looser prohibition on snooping define the kind of political community we are: we are who we are because we do not torture murder suspects—even a suspected serial killer—and do not routinely and pervasively (like Captain Wiesler's Stasi or Big Brother in Orwell's *1984*) observe all of our citizens' doings or listen in on all of their conversations. In our workaday lives here in the West, we like to believe that we strive to be civil, that we would never kidnap or imprison someone, that we abhor violence. And though we expect the police to ask tough questions in an investigation, to arrest and imprison criminals, and to employ force when unavoidable in fulfilling these tasks, we expect—or at least we used to expect—that all this goes only so far, that this toughness has limits. Police ask tough questions but must not use the third degree; they can use deadly force to stop a violent crime but not to stop a thief; the military can bomb and shoot at opposing armies in the field but not use poison gas.

DICK CHENEY, HERO?

But if the existence of the whole community is threatened, do these constraints apply? In the words of the director of the CIA's Counterterrorist Center, Cofer Black, do "the gloves come off?" In the words of Vice President Dick Cheney, the *eminence grise* of counterterrorism policy, do we move "to the dark side"?[3] Do the dictates of conventional morality or even the constraints imposed on the officers of the law and the commanders of the military apply when it comes to safeguarding the welfare of an entire community, when that community might encompass tens or even hundreds of millions of people? For example, consider the testimony of officials responsible for national security in the United States in the days and weeks after 9/11: the daily intelligence reports carried rumors of threats even more catastrophic than the attacks on Washington and New York City.[4] How far may a public servant go in such a situation? How far *must* he go?

This is the problem of "dirty hands." It was Machiavelli's advice to the aspiring ruler that "a man who wishes to profess goodness at all times must fall to ruin among so many who are not good. Whereby it is necessary for a prince who wishes to maintain his position to learn how not to be good, and to use it [goodness] or not according to necessity."[5] By "goodness,"

Machiavelli means all the precepts of conventional morality: telling the truth, being generous, keeping promises, being merciful rather than cruel. But if we live in a world where "so many" do not play by these rules, then to live by them oneself would seem to lead to ruin. Machiavelli admonishes here not the private individual in everyday life but rather "the prince," by which he means anyone with the power and responsibility to rule over a political community. *Necessity* confronts the prince in a form that private morality rarely encounters, because the prince must act for the community as a whole, not merely as a private person.

And so the prince must "learn how not to be good." Machiavelli does *not* say that the prince must learn how to become unabashedly evil or to despise goodness. No sensible person would claim that torture and violation of privacy were things Bush and Cheney had longed to do all along as part of some monstrous craving for power. That the prince must learn "how not to be good" does not mean ceasing to be good at all, but rather learning when and how not to do what is ordinarily thought morally upright, and this seems to capture the willingness to go to the "dark side" when forced. The ruler should know how and when to do what is not ordinarily good, but then only to the extent required by necessity—that is, by the inescapable difference between safety and ruin. Can any political leader or indeed any public servant with substantial responsibility for the community rightly ignore the kind of prudence Machiavelli advises, if success means protecting multitudes of people and failure means their death, enslavement, or similar catastrophe?

In a famous essay on the problem of dirty hands, the political philosopher Michael Walzer took up Machiavelli's argument in a way that scandalized those who had looked to Walzer as a model of moderation and humanity.[6] Can a good person enter the political fray without becoming corrupt or guilty? "My own answer is no," writes Walzer. "I don't think I could govern innocently; nor do most of us believe that those who govern us are innocent . . . even the best of them."[7] On Machiavelli's premise that political life inevitably involves "many who are not good," the answer cannot always be so simple as saying that if you don't want to do wrong, then simply don't. Sometimes achieving a noble purpose will require violating conventional morality, breaking laws. Great purposes and many lives must be at stake; only then may we rightfully break a few eggs to make the omelet. We are not thinking of marginal or technical violations—as in the President's Surveillance Program—but truly horrifying acts: torture, killing of innocents, assassinations, acts that Machiavelli would euphemistically call "not good" but nevertheless necessary. Walzer accepts that we sometimes face tragic choices where we cannot simply keep our hands clean, unless we want to abstain from political life altogether: "But this does not mean that it isn't possible to do the right thing while governing. It means that a particular act of government may be exactly the right thing to do in utilitarian terms and yet leave the man who does it guilty of a moral wrong."[8] For a leader to hold back in a time of great need would not be high-minded virtue but a kind of political cowardice that refuses to accept the responsibility for securing the common good. This refusal to act flees into a purity that is self-serving and selfish.[9] As Max Weber wrote in *Politics as a Vocation*, "He who seeks the salvation of his soul, of his own and of others, should not seek it along the avenue of politics."[10]

But it is conventional morality that instills in people the character and the habits that make them behave well even in terribly stressful situations. It is conventional goodness that teaches a person to work for the sake of the community as a whole if he or she ever comes into a position of responsibility. Machiavelli may say that princes, rulers, public servants must "learn how not to be good" and to use this knowledge only as needed, but that makes it sound like a switch that can be turned on and off. Machiavelli warns that political life cannot go on without immorality and immoral actors. We warn that learning how not to be good either has no beginning or has no end: part of what one unlearns through Machiavelli's teaching is upholding the common good, or any noble ideal, as the aim of political life.[11] And then the goal becomes power for its own sake and the corruption is complete.

So we come to the rare but possible combination of events in which torture truly is the only way to prevent a catastrophe. What then? Given our argument, we must say that the prohibition on torture is an absolute, and so don't do it, no matter what the costs. If the president decides not to torture in the most extreme case, many of those he has assumed responsibility to protect might die. He will have to live with this on his conscience, just as the president who authorizes torture will have that on his conscience. We might want to ask, just how much of their souls do we expect our public servants to sell in dirtying their hands to protect us? Is it right to ask their souls of them, even if it saves lives? What if the most effective way to get a suspect to talk were to torture his innocent child in front of him? Would we ask our public servants to do that for us, no matter the cost to their own consciences?[12] John Yoo, the Justice Department official who together with David Addington, Dick Cheney's chief aide, formulated the legal justification for the president's extraordinary claims, thought yes. In a debate after he left office he was asked, "If the President deems that he's got to torture somebody, including by crushing the testicles of the person's child, there is no law that can stop him?" And Yoo replied, "I think it depends on why he thinks he needs to do that."[13] It would be difficult to find a more bloodless embrace of atrocity justified by executive supremacy and *raison d'état*.

If it is the leader's ultimate responsibility to be prepared to lose even his soul in a cause that all can understand, then his may be the most extreme, the most costly kind of moral heroism. But at some point, the world will perish and the heavens will fall. Must they take our souls with them? This is what Machiavelli forced us to confront as the dilemma of dirty hands. Machiavelli indeed celebrated the citizens of Florence who loved their city more than their immortal souls and were willing to brave excommunication in defying the orders of the pope.

We squirm and seek a middle way where there is none. To be torn is not a solution to the paradox. We cannot heave a sigh of relief and say, "Oh, we cannot have it both ways, but we must; so it's all alright after all." To recognize and accept, as did the ancient Greeks, the tragedy of living in a broken world where goodness and virtue do not always prevail, will not turn tragedy into romantic comedy with a happy ending. The tragedy remains. The good man who tries to temper necessity with decency might be a hero with dirty hands, but he is a tragic hero. To be human, to be a *human* political animal means we must confront this tragedy with open eyes or else give up on goodness altogether and give in to the absolute corruption of wielding power for its own sake. It means at least making decency, not perfect goodness, the touchstone of the political vocation: goodness that upholds all the ideals of law and morals, that embraces perfect morality but—like a soldier leaving his wife as he goes off to war—loosens that embrace to avoid seeing the common good come to ruin. It means a sadder but wiser prudence.

The Machiavellian ruler has no sense of tragedy. Harry Truman is reported to have said that (unlike J. Robert Oppenheimer and Secretary of War Henry Stimson) he never lost a night's sleep over his decision to drop the atom bomb.[14] Machiavelli's tone is closer to triumphant and even cheerful than soberly regretful about the tragic necessities of political life. He seems to celebrate some of the most unscrupulous leaders in history, men who make their own glory, which they regularly proclaim is the good and glory of their community too, the polestar of their ambition.[15] But the twentieth century taught us that the ruler unhinged from all traditional notions of morality is the greatest curse: Hitler, Stalin, Pol Pot—they show us how far the Devil can go when all the laws are cut down and the ruler is unleashed with nearly absolute power.

Once a political community makes that kind of power available, perhaps as a desperate last resort in a time of crisis, it is all too likely that a monster will appear to seize it, however careful or careless his predecessors were in circumscribing it, because that kind of power by its very nature knows no bounds. Learning how not to be good while at the same time retaining goodness as the ultimate guide for decent action is an almost unimaginably difficult balancing act. And yet that act is precisely what the tragedy of the human condition demands.[16] At least, when times are hard. This is the grim metric we must apply when judging the actions of the Bush administration, to discern whether they kept to the right side of tragedy or lurched into hubris.

SQUARING THE CIRCLE

Squaring the circle is an operation that cannot be performed— at least not with mathematical (geometric) precision, but only by successive approximations. Can it be performed at all— must we choose between guilt and ruin? What follows is as close as we can get.

First, there are actions that though illegal are not indecent. They are wrong because they are illegal; they are not illegal because they are wrong. Some of the illegal actions taken after 9/11 (aspects of the surveillance program, the temporary detentions of aliens) are quite analogous to Jefferson's and Lincoln's illegal actions taken in response to the crises they faced, and the actions of these two great presidents are a model for squaring this particular circle. It is a model that analogizes executive lawbreaking to civil disobedience. Civil disobedience comes in two strands. One professes a fundamental allegiance to the political community and its system of laws and government, but holds that if some laws are such an affront to the conscience of its citizens, it is the citizens' right and duty to disobey these laws in an attempt to change them. This was Martin Luther King Jr.'s strategy. The other strand has no such allegiance to the system; instead, it uses the techniques of nonviolent action and lawbreaking to overthrow the existing government.[17] The first focuses on reform, the second on revolution. The former is civil disobedience proper; the latter is nonviolent political action. As Locke and the American founders recognized, tyranny may well justify revolution. Given our focus in this chapter on executive lawbreaking (that is, lawbreaking by those who enjoy constitutional authority), the second strand would be not revolution but a coup d'état. Executive disobedience is analogous to the first, which professes (as did Jefferson and Lincoln) a fundamental loyalty to the state and its laws.

It is crucial to civil disobedience that its practitioners, in disobeying the law, do so in a civil manner. *Civil* here does not just mean "polite," although Gandhi and King stressed the importance of resolute courtesy when engaging in principled lawbreaking because the opponent is someone with whom, in principle, one expects to reconcile in a more just community once the conflict has been resolved. What *civil* refers to, then, is the bond that the lawbreakers maintain with a political community united by a sense that it is one people, rather than a mere accumulation of disconnected individuals, families, or groups. As a people, it shares a common good, recognizes the basic justice of its constitution and civil institutions, and accepts the rule of law as well as the existing system of laws as binding on the citizen body as a whole.

Civil disobedience accepts the legitimacy of the law and the rule of law in general, but, in effect, it relies on the Lockean idea that no sovereign, even one appointed by the people itself, can be so wise as never to commit a serious error in making law. Some laws will be not merely imprudent or silly, but deeply wrong, contrary to the fundamental principles and interests that united the people as a people in the first place and that transcend any specific law. Civil disobedience breaks those specific laws to focus the attention of the people as a whole on the injustice of those laws; for example, the civil rights movement in the United States used sit-ins to call attention to the injustice of Jim Crow laws. Because civil disobedience seeks the rectification of the law and the redemption of the principles that unite society, its practitioners are civil in the usual sense: in breaking the law, they take pains not to offend or insult their fellow citizens because they are seeking to reconcile and heal a wound in the body politic embodied by the unjust law.

They are civil in a more specific sense: they break the law in a way that emphasizes their allegiance to the rule of law and the existing system of laws and institutions in general, with the exception of the law or set of laws in question. They break the law openly, often declaring their intention to do so in advance. They break the law reluctantly only for reasons of deep principle and in situations of great urgency, after making a good faith effort to change the law by legal means. They do not resist or avoid the representatives of the state when they arrest them. The practitioners resist by pleading their case in court, because they affirm the system they share with fellow citizens, and they accept their punishment if the court goes against them for the same reason, trusting that their fellow citizens will see the light eventually.

All this requires a civic courage and a civic sense of honor: to take a risk for the greater good of the community and its fundamental, unifying principles. Consider the case of Henry Brown and four friends, all black, who entered the library of Clinton, Louisiana, which was designated for whites only. Brown requested a book, *The Story of the Negro*, and when he was told that the library did not have it but would order it, all five young men quietly sat down and refused to leave. They were arrested and prosecuted for disturbing the peace, although they had done no more than cross the color line of segregation. They accepted this legal burden willingly, with the faith that the law of the land would vindicate them. They took their case to the Supreme Court, and they won, but they won not only for themselves.[18] Their civic, civil disobedience was just one among the acts of many thousands of other citizens who broke a local, but ultimately unjust law in order to desegregate the nation and to uphold its ideals. Those practicing civil disobedience willingly take on risks for the same reason that a soldier does: to protect the fundamental principles of the society and to preserve the unity of the body politic. There is honor, even nobility, to both forms of risk taking.

Now, consider the examples put forward already of executives acting unconstitutionally in times of crisis: Jefferson assuming powers of the Congress after the *Chesapeake* affair; Lincoln doing the same at the outbreak of civil war. Is lawbreaking by officers of the government, at least in some cases, analogous to civil disobedience? We might call this executive disobedience, or as Oren Gross has called it, official disobedience.[19] At first blush, the analogy does not seem to hold, because the disobedient official is someone who has taken an oath to uphold the law. This is the oath that the Constitution prescribes for the president: "I do solemnly swear (or affirm) that I will faithfully execute the Office of President of the United States, and will to the best of my Ability, preserve, protect and defend the Constitution of the United States." Note that the oath does not mention defending national security; the president's duty is explicitly to the law, not some vague goal beyond the law. Indeed, Article VI of the Constitution requires that "all executive and judicial Officers both of the United States and the several states shall be bound by Oath or Affirmation to support the Constitution." Presidents are public servants precisely because they serve the public interest as embodied by law; for the law is the expression of the people's will that such officers "execute." If a public servant is unhappy with this, if performing his legal duties deeply violates his conscience, he should resign.

This makes it seem like the analogy between civil disobedience and executive lawbreaking is doomed from the start. A judge or prosecutor or president or police officer who considers a specific law profoundly unjust should not simply disregard that law, refuse to act on it, or actively break it. She should either uphold the law or step down, for she acts not on her own authority but on public trust. Disobedience to law is therefore profoundly antithetical to the very role of a public servant, who is entrusted with power not only to obey the law but also to uphold and defend it.

But this ignores the point made by Aristotle and Locke: that the law cannot always foresee what is in the public interest. It is not because the police officer or the president sees that the law is unjust that she bends or breaks it, but because she sees that it is inadequate to the specific case at hand. The official might break the law, not because it would be gravely unjust to uphold it under any circumstances (she should resign if that is what she thinks), but because it would be prudent and reasonable (in the sense of Aristotle's *epieikeia*) to prevent the letter of the law from causing a grave injustice in a particular, unanticipated case.

Imagine the police officer who broke some laws in order to get your loved one to the hospital in an emergency: she reports to her chief the next day, explains what she has done, puts her badge and gun on the chief's desk, and waits for a response. Both Jefferson after provisioning the military and Lincoln after suspending habeas corpus asked Congress to cure the defect retroactively by passing the laws there was no time to pass originally. After all, congressional action at the outset would have removed any illegality. All that is left is the fact that the actions were illegal in the interim, but to insist on that is not fidelity to law but rule-fetishism, the opposite of Aristotle's *epieikeia*. Similarly, we can also say that parts of the

President's Surveillance Program were wrong only because they were illegal—they violated FISA—and that Congress's action in 2008 in passing the FISA Amendments Act cured that defect. Indeed, Congress went further and immunized those whose actions were illegal when they did them, but were illegal no longer.[20]

But what if Congress declines to ratify what the president has done? He can then up the ante: he presents his own articles of impeachment, detailing the laws broken as well as presenting his reasons for breaking them. Impeachment of the president is a rare and serious event, and this voluntary first step by the president would repeat on a grand scale the police officer's gesture in handing in her badge and gun. Only two presidents have been impeached: Andrew Johnson, for disregarding the Tenure of Office Act, requiring him to submit dismissals of cabinet officers for Senate approval—a requirement thought to be unconstitutional since the Decision of 1789;[21] and then Bill Clinton, an impeachment that (to paraphrase Marx) repeated what in Johnson's case was tragedy, this time as farce. Both impeachments failed in the Senate.

Our system is reluctant to impeach the president. Nonetheless, a president who has acted against established law, for what he believes to be a proper purpose and in defiance of Congress, should invoke the Constitution's ultimate judgment by inviting Congress to treat his lawbreaking as a "high crime or misdemeanor," just as those engaging in civil disobedience in effect dare the authorities to arrest them. The president runs a risk in doing this, of course, but leadership requires that pledge of "sacred Honor" in exercising one's highest responsibilities. The civic daring required here is simply the proper move in a constitutional system where the rule of law is paramount, but where that very respect for law may endanger the community and the system of law as a whole. But when there is a breach in the rule of law, then it is the duty of the official responsible to heal that breach by being explicit about what has happened and exposing himself to the law. This is the honorable thing to do, for it demonstrates respect for the law, even in the breach.

In his letter on the *Chesapeake* affair, Jefferson recognized that in an emergency, public servants must hold to the principle that the welfare of the people trumps the letter of the written law. "The officer who is called to act on this superior ground, does indeed risk himself on the justice of the controlling powers of the constitution, and his station makes it his duty to incur that risk."[22] The risk Jefferson refers to here is not physical danger but rather the moral risk of prosecution or disgrace. A public servant must therefore take office fully aware of the need for courage to assume this risk, because there might come times when a crisis will require him to bend or break the law, and then the institutions of the government might well hold him liable after the fact. Jefferson ran that risk in the *Chesapeake* affair, when he assumed powers of the purse assigned to Congress, but he placed his faith in the people, and so in their representatives forgiving the breach by an officer of the law who acted with honor and good faith during an evident crisis. As long as the act is limited in scope and duration and is openly acknowledged by the officer as a temporary departure from the normal operation of the rule of law, the modern executive should have the same expectation. But to refuse to acknowledge the breach, to act as if it were the prerogative of power, is to enter on the path of despotism.

To round out the analogy, both civil and executive disobedience operate on the foundation of an allegiance to the rule of law and the institutions of civil society. Just as civil disobedience, then, will not break the law frivolously or hastily, executive disobedience will break the law only under emergency conditions when all other options have been exhausted (although in a true emergency, sometimes the time for exploring other options may be desperately short). This means the officer will break only the specific laws that pertain to the emergency at hand; he will not consider himself to be above the law generally, free to pick and choose at will. Civil disobedience requires that its practitioners act openly, although sometimes this might not be immediately possible in the case of executive disobedience, for instance, if the emergency is one that requires secrecy. At least the details of the President's Surveillance Program following 9/11 might fit this description.

There is a great danger to secret executive lawbreaking. What is done in secret, with all the power of the executive behind it, could metastasize into the arbitrary, lawless power of the tyrant—as it did in the Weimar Republic, with Hitler's rise to power. It is crucial, then, that executives keep clear records of their lawbreaking, not just as part of their regular logs and journals, but in a distinct and explicit chronicle of the actions taken that might reasonably be construed as a breach of the rule of law, a chronicle intended for public revelation as soon as the immediate crisis is over. And even during the events, they must share their immediate secrets with some in another branch of government, for in a republic worth saving, the executive and its servants cannot be the only ones trusted. After all, the emergency may never seem to be over, and then the power of the executive will grow more and more dictatorial. The Bush administration not only showed no inclination to make public its extraordinary decisions, but also proclaimed that no act performed by the president in his capacity as commander in chief could be construed as lawbreaking at all. When cornered, the administration sent Attorney General Alberto Gonzales to Congress to offer testimony so clumsily evasive as to mock the very notion of democratic oversight.[23]

Whenever we admit that executive authorities can break the laws they are entrusted to uphold, we are in dangerous territory. Executive disobedience requires an even more stringent justification than civil disobedience. Those practicing civil disobedience accept that the agents of civil society (the police, prosecutors, etc.) have the right to arrest and bring them to trial. Again: the executive who disobeys the law should, when the emergency is past, not only make public the record of the lawbreaking but also present herself for disciplinary action, with the honorable hope but not the arrogant expectation that the breach will be forgiven. And so the executive does not arrogate to herself the presumption of Aristotle's ideal monarch: a wisdom that admits no challenge to its authority because that wisdom is putatively complete and beyond the ken of ordinary citizens. We are back to Locke's modern skepticism about whether any ruler can embody such a nearly perfect wisdom; institutions and law must check arbitrary power.

One might ask, how can we expect officers of our government to do what is needed for our welfare when that might call for breaking some laws, if afterward they must expose themselves to dismissal, resignation, or even prosecution?[24] Indeed, our proposal is that they themselves take the initiative in calling attention to the laws they have broken, without waiting for others to force action. But won't this requirement have a chilling effect so that those in positions of authority will not do what necessity requires when our national security is at stake? We must listen to Locke's warning that the reign of excellent and effective princes who transcend the law is a great danger to a people's liberty. A chilling effect is exactly what we need when it comes to the rule of law. And we must ask our executive officers to demonstrate a civic version of the virtue that we ask of our soldiers, who risk so much more in defending the country. This is the pledge of sacred honor evoked by the founders, and the necessity of civic risk identified by Jefferson. After all, we know this is possible, because practitioners of civil disobedience accept this same risk of prosecution.

THE CIRCLE WON'T SQUARE

Our analogy between executive disobedience and civil disobedience works quite well as applied to the President's Surveillance Program under Bush. The claim would be similar to Lincoln's and Jefferson's justifications for their extralegal actions. All three presidents could contemplate a retroactive wiping clean of the slate if Congress ratified their judgments. But the interrogation program urged by Vice President Cheney (in Cofer Black's words, now "the gloves come off")[25] and the notorious Yoo memos defining away the reality of torture in order to justify and immunize it are of quite a different order. It is not as if the statutes and treaties banning torture and cruel, inhuman, and degrading treatment were inadequately drafted or failed to imagine novel circumstances (as with FISA). There was nothing at all novel about the need to extract information from unwilling prisoners; nor, on the controversial analogy to war, was there anything novel about the imperatives to identify and prevent attacks by clandestine enemy agents. The prohibitions against torture and cruel, inhuman, and degrading treatment were written for just such situations.

Eavesdropping, provisioning the army without statutory warrant, even arresting and holding suspected enemy aliens are of an entirely different order. Laws might be drafted (after the fact, if need be) and compensation paid[26] to cover such actions. For torture, never. As we have said, eavesdropping is wrong because it is illegal. Torture is illegal because it is wrong. And when a public official tortures, that is when his hands are dirty indeed—it is more than just a little dirt under his fingernails. Confession and asking for retroactive validation will not do. There must be a more radical response, not just formal erasure. There must be justice, condemnation, disgrace. To hesitate, to draw back is to condone and to make us all accomplices after the fact of moral abomination.

In the case of "mere" lawbreaking—Jefferson, Lincoln,

electronic surveillance—if the acts had gone unratified, the president would be a criminal. That is the risk he ran. Though he is legally liable to be treated as a criminal, and punished as one, no dictate of law or of morality forces us to prosecute or punish him, since no dictate of law or morality requires that every criminal act be prosecuted and punished. In our system of justice, prosecutors have discretion, and they exercise it on our behalf. Indeed, the Constitution requires that prosecutions for serious crimes go forward only if a grand jury indicts, and grand juries need not explain why they choose not to indict. (One of the more fatuous arguments for the impeachment of Bill Clinton was that he had after all perjured himself—a felony—and therefore impeachment must follow.)

The invocation of prosecutorial discretion works well for violations of statutory law, later ratified by Congress. And even if Congress refuses to condone the violation (if the president is unpopular or his policy has failed), perhaps that repudiation itself vindicates the law. But we consider torture a crime that no later ratification can erase. If we do not condemn, prosecute, punish the torturers and those who ordered them to torture, we become accomplices after the fact. But of course on Walzer's and Machiavelli's account we are indeed accomplices after the fact. Horrors were committed to keep us safe. Prosecutorial discretion is a part of our system, but is its exercise here not just a further offense against morality? Should the president and his subordinates—the vice president, his counsel, and his collaborators—not pay for their moral "heroism" in doing our dirty work for us? History has examples that point both ways. The Nuremberg War Crimes Trials accomplished a great deal in publicizing and punishing the crimes of the Nazi regime. They serve as the name for a calm, dignified, and probing retribution. And they headed off the much more summary retribution that the Nazi leadership would otherwise have faced.[27] The monsters heard their victims accuse them. The victors had to make a case. The accused were allowed to defend themselves. The same can be said of the tribunals for the atrocities committed during the wars in the former Yugoslavia, for the genocide in Rwanda, and for the remnants of the Khmer Rouge.[28]

But President Truman and General Curtis LeMay were never prosecuted for ordering the firebombings of Tokyo or for Hiroshima and Nagasaki. Sir Arthur Harris, "Bomber" Harris, was never prosecuted for the firebombing of Dresden and other German cities. William Ranney Levi recently collected the great deal that is known but never discussed about brutal interrogation techniques used by the CIA since at least 1951.[29] Project Artichoke focused on the use of a wide variety of little understood drugs; heat, cold, isolation, and "electric" methods were in use as early as the early 1960s. And "President Truman reportedly provided Walter Bedell Smith, CIA director from 1951–1953, a blanket and undated presidential pardon when concerns about legality began to trouble Smith."[30] But even the promise of a retroactive pardon at least concedes that crimes might have been committed, and therefore concedes that the law is something the chief executive is bound to take into account. It is another thing, as the Bush administration has done, to argue that a president's directives can never result in crimes on the grounds that whatever the president orders, in his role as commander in chief, is for that reason lawful, whatever laws those acts might seem to break.

Is there talk of prosecuting Bush and Cheney and Gonzales and Yoo only because it is far from clear that their tactics have succeeded? If we had quickly captured Osama bin Laden and Mullah Omar, found weapons of mass destruction, and left a peaceful, prosperous Afghanistan and Iraq, would these inquests and questions have attained any traction? If there is only victors' justice,[31] then the condemnation of torture means next to nothing, and we practice restraint only because we fear the consequences in case we lose. The cry of "victors' justice" was of course Goering's complaint at Nuremberg: that only the Germans were being singled out for atrocities committed by both sides. The only response to Goering—and it is not an adequate one—is essentially this: victory makes justice possible, of course, but not all justice is the same, and certainly not all victors' justice is the same. Would you want the Nazis as victors putting you on trial, or the Allies? The proceedings would not have had the calm dignity of Nuremberg, the meticulous presentation of evidence, the scrupulous regard for the accuseds' right to put on as full a defense as they chose.

If there is only victors' justice, that would mean in effect that torture is not wrong, but only torturing and losing. So must we prosecute to make the point? The Bush administration broke the law in ordering torture, mocked the Constitution in its interpretation of executive authority, and outraged common decency. Must there not be prosecutions to reaffirm constitutional limits on the executive and lift the cloud of complicity from us all? In working on this book together, we have talked through to agreement every other issue we have addressed, but this one leaves us at an impasse.

One of us, Gregory, thinks that restoring our constitutional and moral integrity requires that these loose ends be tied, and that knitting up can only be accomplished by treating the culprits as the criminals they are—Machiavellian heroes though they may be. First, it is patently unjust that low-level lawbreakers be prosecuted for overstepping (sometimes by a wide margin) their orders from above, while the officials who issued those orders, knowing they were a perversion of their authority, are not. And yet that has happened. In a democratic republic committed to the rule of law, such double standards, with high officials left free to act above the law, can have just as corrosive an effect on the public trust as vindictiveness, between parties in and out of power, knifing each other back and forth through politically motivated impeachments and prosecutions. Furthermore, in cases where executive lawbreaking sets a dangerous precedent—both in terms of the expansion of dictatorial powers and in terms of effectively legalizing torture—the failure to prosecute risks leaving that precedent in place, implicitly ratifying it. Finally, to the extent that the United States or any democratic republic wishes to exert pressure on countries where the rule of law is only developing, failing to hold our own leaders accountable for their crimes when it proves awkward sets a lamentable example.

This last point also underlines a theme we have touched

on throughout this book: that democratic governments and decent communities rely on certain shared understandings about what kinds of actions are simply beyond the pale. This is at bottom a conservative, Burkean argument about national character and how devastating it can be to meddle with shared ethical instincts cultivated over generations: to encroach on fundamental taboos, even when the usefulness of torture, for example, might seem clear in a particular case, is to risk eroding the grounding moral habits of the people, their government, and its officials. Torture is the habit of tyranny, not of free republics, and it cannot simply be switched on and off. It inculcates a conception of state power and human worth that directly conflicts with our founding principle of an inalienable dignity to the human person, even the most culpable. As we know from Abu Ghraib, once it is unleashed, even as a supposedly well-quarantined tactic practiced by putative professionals, torture spreads like cancer. Today, some argue that we should torture the enemy only in ticking-bomb scenarios, as a way to save lives. But tomorrow, why not torture all enemy prisoners to get information that might also save lives? And then why not torture citizen criminals here at home, if that too might save lives? This is the lesson of history for all governments that turn to torture: an isolated practice expands to become the emblem of state power and the reality of the citizens' subjection. Although the force of our argument against torture is a deontological one, this particular point stresses what we might become if we give up on the absolute prohibition against torture. Prosecution of those responsible, not just hapless subordinates far down the chain of command, would reassert the salutary vigor of a taboo essential to a democratic nation.

In the United States the decision to go forward with such prosecutions is ultimately political. The actual decision will be taken by the attorney general, who serves at the pleasure of the president (as President Richard Nixon's firing of Attorney General Elliot Richardson and Deputy Attorney General William Ruckelshaus for not firing special Watergate prosecutor Archibald Cox demonstrated) by tradition and conscience but is supposed to come to prosecution decisions independently. President Obama invoked that tradition in referring the question of criminal investigation and prosecution to Attorney General Eric Holder. But that only moves the politics one step down the line of authority; it does not remove it. In our system the attorney general, or state district attorneys, have discretion in choosing what to investigate and whom to prosecute. (In some other nations it is said that the prosecuting authorities have no choice but to prosecute crime, especially serious crime, when it has come to their attention. That is not our system and the one step in that direction, the independent counsel law, was widely seen as a disaster, ending in the Clinton-Lewinsky-Whitewater debacle.) Once again, this is a political decision in the highest sense, and the use of that political discretion is accountable to the people and only to them. So how should the attorney general decide? His decision must depend on how far the high officials concerned went in breaking the law, and there is still very much that we do not know. But we should know, and both public officials and private citizens should insist on knowing, what has been done in our name. But if we are to assume the worst, only criminal prosecution and conviction proclaim in the clearest terms that what was done was a high crime, that no one, not even the president, has the authority to commit such crimes in our name. Since the beginning of government, criminal condemnation has been societies' sharpest form of rebuke and their definitive disassociation with the crime.

The other of us, Charles, is not so sure. The option for prosecution for high officials should remain open—there should be no pardons—at issue here is a practical point about maintaining faith in a democracy. One of the strengths of successful, long-standing republics has been the peaceful transfer of power between sworn political enemies. That has not been the rule always and everywhere. Far more usual in other types of regimes has been the severe and vengeful punishment, killing, banishment, or dispossession of the leaders of the outgoing regime by the new. This was true at the restoration of democracy after the ouster of the oligarchs in Athens, the Terror in France, Stalin's purges, Hitler's night of the long knives. Where the incoming party has shown restraint—not only Napoleon, the Bourbon Restoration, the Restoration in England, but also the establishment of democracy in Spain after the death of Franco, and most shiningly in the behavior of the Mandela-led new South Africa after the dismantling of apartheid—this was seen as a sign of strength and confidence, not weakness, and led to stability.

That is why the criminal prosecution of the leaders of the defeated administration unsettles the body politic. Surely those prosecuted today, or their loyal partisans, will turn in fury on the prosecutors when it comes their turn to throw the rascals out. This not only undermines the public notion that disagreements are settled at the ballot box and not in the courtroom, but also has a bad effect on the incoming regime. The new leaders might be more timid than they should be, fearing retribution when their turn comes; or they will have a motive to cling to power as long as and as fiercely as possible in order to stave off the evil day. This unsettling melody has played itself out in a minor and key and muted way by the series of independent counsel prosecutions following the ouster of Nixon. The Republicans were aching to go after the Carter people—the highest they aimed at were Billy Carter and Jody Powell, and both of those were misses. The pursuit by a Democratic Congress after 1986 of high-level Reagan officials was followed by the black comedy of the Whitewater and Lewinsky prosecutions and the debacle of the Clinton impeachment. To the public, these episodes began to look not like high-minded vindications of respect for law, but rather like politics masquerading as law—and therefore sordid and vengeful. We can see why President Obama has said he does not want to rake up the past. Everyone has or eventually will have a past.

Whether to prosecute or not should depend on many things: the scale of the transgression—Cheney is not Hitler, Stalin, Mao, Pol Pot—the depth of the crimes, their essentially defensive motivation and context. After all, the Bush administration was protecting us against an enemy for whom killing and maiming innocents was the signature technique. All these factors weigh in favor of our torturers in this instance. We are in the realm not of justification—the acts cannot be justified—but of excuse. The administration of justice excuses those who have acted wrongly under unbearable pressure. Our argument about the absolute wrong of torture holds even if we excuse someone who has done it in a moment of terrible emergency; to excuse an isolated act is not to endorse that act, and it certainly is not to validate a whole regime of "enhanced interrogation" as a matter of settled policy. As much as we might wish to see all wrongdoers brought to justice, that general expectation is not always just in individual cases. And so prosecutors do not always prosecute, grand juries do not always indict nor trial juries convict when they believe the defendant should be excused, even if a crime has been committed. Furthermore, a failed prosecution would come at a greater cost to our nation and our decency than leaving the crimes unprosecuted. Weighing against the offenders is their arrogance, their mendacity, and their perversion of constitutional government.

Finally, there is the question, what alternatives are there? The possibility of prosecution should continue to hang over their heads—there should be no immunity. Also, as they purported to act in our name and in our defense, there should be an accounting, exposure, and repudiation. As Gross has noted, Bomber Harris's command never received a campaign medal, as did the men of the Fighter Command, although Bomber Command lost over fifty-seven thousand men. The use of poison gas in World War I led to its being outlawed, its hardly being used in World War II, and those who ordered its use in Iraq being hanged.[32] And atomic weapons have not been used in the six decades since Hiroshima and Nagasaki.

Thomas More was right that unwavering insistence on the law is a shield against tyrannical power; but in prosecutions and punishment the law works not as a shield but as a sword. The decision to swing that sword, the decisions whether to prosecute or punish are questions of prudence, discretion, Aristotle's *epieikeia*. Here the hero is not Dick Cheney but Nelson Mandela.

NOTES

INTRODUCTION

1. *Das Leben der Anderen*, Florian Henckel von Donnersmarck (2006).

2. The image of God is used to explicate Locke's conception of human equality in Jeremy Waldron, *God, Locke and Equality: Christian Foundations of Locke's Political Thought* (Cambridge: Cambridge University Press, 2002), and by George Fletcher in "In God's Image: The Religious Imperative of Equality under Law," 99 *Columbia Law Review* 1608 (1999). In *Tort Liability for Human Rights Abuses* (Oxford: Hart, 2008), ch. 5 and especially p. 121 n. 17 and accompanying text, Fletcher makes the connection between the concepts of equality, human dignity, and the prohibition on torture.

ABSOLUTELY WRONG

1. Convention Against Torture and Other Cruel, Inhuman or Degrading Treatment or Punishment, 14 GS U.N.T.S. 85 (1984). See the essays collected in anthologies such as *Torture: A Collection*, Sanford Levinson, ed. (New York: Oxford University Press, 2004), and *The Phenomenon of Torture:*

Readings and Commentary, William F. Schulz, ed. (Philadelphia: University of Pennsylvania Press, 2007).

2. Richard Bernstein, "Kidnapping Has Germans Debating Police Torture," *New York Times*, April 10, 2003, p. A3, and John Hooper, "Kidnap Case Presents Germans with Ugly Dilemma over Torture," *Guardian*, February 27, 2003, p. 18.

3. Alan Dershowitz, *Why Terrorism Works: Understanding the Threat, Responding to the Challenge* (New Haven: Yale University Press, 2002).

4. Richard Posner, "Torture, Terrorism, and Interrogation," in *Torture: A Collection*, Sanford Levinson, ed. (New York: Oxford University Press, 2004), pp. 296–97.

5. Jeremy Waldron, "Jurisprudence for the White House," 105 *Columbia Law Review* 1681, 1726–27 (2005).

6. Piero della Francesca, *The Flagellation*, 1469, Galleria Nazionale delle Marche, Urbino.

7. Shakespeare, *Hamlet*, Act 2, scene 2, lines 307–10. The same point is movingly made by Ronald Dworkin, *Life's Dominion: An Argument about Abortion, Euthanasia, and Individual Freedom* ("The Sanctity of Each Human Life") (New York: Alfred A. Knopf, 1993), pp. 81–84.

8. See Robert Nozick's comparison between two types of moral constraints: those that require an overall minimization of rights violations, and those that operate as side constraints prohibiting some actions regardless of the utilitarian consequences. See his *Anarchy, State, and Utopia* (New York: Basic Books, 1974), pp. 26–35.

9. Baruch Spinoza speaks of a living being's conatus (see his *Ethics*, James Gutman, ed. [New York: Hafner, 1949]) (1677),

and Gottfried Leibniz of its appetite for survival. Whether or not there is such a conatus, the Darwinian argument is only contingently coincidental with it, and under certain conditions as an actual disposition it does not obtain at all. Roger Ariew and Daniel Garber's collection of Leibniz essays (*Philosophical Essays* [Indianapolis: Hackett, 1989]) contains the 1695 work "A Specimen of Dynamics" (pp. 117–37) in which Leibniz discusses conatus and its role in the motion of bodies. Garber discusses conatus in his essay "Motion and Metaphysics in the Young Leibniz" in Michael Hooker's *Leibniz: Critical and Interpretive Essays* (Minneapolis: University of Minnesota Press, 1982). Finally, Laurence Carlin has a relatively recent paper titled "Leibniz on Conatus, Causation, and Freedom," *Pacific Philosophical Quarterly*, vol. 85, no. 4 (2004), pp. 365–79. Our thanks to Brian Kiniry for these references.

10. Address to Special Session of Congress (July 4, 1861) in *The Collected Works of Abraham Lincoln* (New Brunswick, NJ: Rutgers University Press, 1953), vol. 4, pp. 421, 430.

11. See Ludwig Wittgenstein, *Philosophical Investigations*, G. E. M. Anscombe, trans. (New York: Macmillan, 1953), sect. 217.

12. This is an obvious and intended reformulation of the Kantian proposition that the ultimate moral commitment is to humanity in our own person and in every person, and that humanity consists of the very capacity for moral judgment and commitment. (Compare this to the Benthamite utilitarian bedrock principle that pleasure and pain are the ultimate values and so the capacity of every being to feel these—to the degree that every being can feel them—acquires moral significance.)

BORDERING ON TORTURE

1. See U.S. Department of Defense, *Working Group Report on Detainee Interrogations in the Global War on Terrorism: Assessment of Legal, Historical, Policy and Operational Considerations* (April 4, 2003), reprinted in *The Torture Papers: The Road to Abu Ghraib*, Karen J. Greenberg and Joshua L. Dratel, eds. (Cambridge: Cambridge University Press, 2005), p. 286, for an inventory of some of these techniques. The August 1, 2004, opinion from the Office of Legal Counsel also discusses many means of interrogation and includes an appendix describing the facts of U.S. cases in which courts have concluded the defendant tortured the plaintiff. Memorandum from Jay S. Bybee, Assistant Attorney General, Office of Legal Counsel, to Alberto R. Gonzales, Counsel to the President, "Re: Standards of Conduct for Interrogation under 18 U.S.C. §§2340–2340A" (called the "Bybee Memo"), in *The Torture Papers*, Greenberg and Dratel, eds., pp. 172–217.

2. We do not consider offers of favors to which the subject is not otherwise entitled—that is, an offer that improves the subject's situation relative to what it would be had there been no contact with him. See Robert Nozick, "Coercion," in *Philosophy, Science, and Method*, Sydney Morgenbesser et al., eds. (New York: St. Martin's Press, 1969).

3. There is an extensive philosophical literature on this topic, deriving from Judith Jarvis Thomson's canonical posing of the "trolley problem": an out-of-control trolley is hurtling down a track, bound to kill five people. Should I throw a switch that

will turn it onto another track, where it will just as surely kill one person? Judith Jarvis Thomson, "The Trolley Problem," 94 *Yale Law Journal* 1395 (1985). Francis Kamm's aptly named *Intricate Ethics* (Oxford: Oxford University Press, 2007) is a recent exploration of this and related dilemmas, many drawn from situations that arise in warfare. Kamm's book has a comprehensive annotation to the literature on pp. 24–26.

4. Here our account is similar to Elaine Scarry's in ch. 2 of her book *The Body in Pain: The Making and Unmaking of the World* (New York: Oxford University Press, 1985).

5. A variant might claim that it is not human life that is of inestimable value but rather that taking a life is categorically and nonnegotiably wrong, so that the victim only violates the injunction by killing and not at all by allowing the aggressor to kill him. But what is the principle behind that?

6. See Jane Mayer's opening description in "The Predator War," *New Yorker*, October 26, 2009, pp. 36–45.

7. Article 27 of the Fourth Geneva Convention states, "Protected persons are entitled, in all circumstances, to respect for their persons, their honour, their family rights, their religious convictions and practices, and their manners and customs. They shall at all times be humanely treated, and shall be protected especially against all acts of violence or threats thereof and against insults and public curiosity." Article 31 states, "No physical or moral coercion shall be exercised against protected persons, in particular to obtain information from them or from third parties."

Article 17 of the Third Geneva Convention, on POWs, stipulates, "Every prisoner of war, when questioned on the subject, is bound to give only his surname, first names and rank, date of birth, and army, regimental, personal or serial number, or failing this, equivalent information . . . No physical or mental torture, nor any other form of coercion, may be inflicted on prisoners of war to secure from them information of any kind whatever. Prisoners of war who refuse to answer may not be threatened, insulted, or exposed to unpleasant or disadvantageous treatment of any kind."

8. A commission in the 1980s examining Israel's interrogation techniques concluded that "moderate physical pressure" may be permissible when it did not rise to the level of torture, but the precise techniques allowed were only specified in a second, classified section. *Report of Commission of Inquiry into the Methods of Investigation of the General Security Service Regarding Hostile Terrorist Activity, First Part* (Jerusalem, October 1987), reprinted in 23 *Israel Law Review* 146 (1989). In H.C. 5100/94 *Pub. Comm. Against Torture v. Israel*, 53(4) P.D. 817 (1999), the Israeli Supreme Court prohibited the use of several stress positions—including the "shabach" and "frog crouch" positions.

9. In an essay published posthumously, John Rawls described his experiences in World War II as a turning point in his conception of the relationship between religion and morality. See "On My Religion," in *A Brief Inquiry into the Meaning of Sin and Faith: With "On My Religion"* (Cambridge, MA: Harvard University Press, 2009).

10. This is the phrase of Cofer Black, the director of the CIA's Counterterrorist Center. Joint House/Senate Intelligence Commitee Hearing, Testimony of Cofer Black

(September 26, 2002), available at www.fas.org/irp/con
gress/2002_hr/092602black.html.

11. Official reports include the *Senate Armed Services Committee
Inquiry into the Treatment of Detainees in U.S. Custody*,
(December 11 2008), xxvi–xxix, available at http://armed-
services.senate.gov/Publications/EXEC%20SUMMARY
-CONCLUSIONS_For%20Release_12%20December%20
2008.pdf, and U.S. Department of Defense, *Army Regulation
15–6: Final Report: Investigation into the FBI Allegations of
Detainee Abuse at Guantanamo Bay, Cuba Detention Facility*,
13–18 (April 1, 2005, amended June 9, 2005), available at
http://www.defenselink.mil/news/Jul2005/d20050714report.
pdf. See also Jane Mayer, *The Dark Side: The Inside Story of
How the War on Terror Turned into a War on American Ideals*
(New York: Doubleday, 2008); *The Torture Papers*, Greenberg
and Dratel, eds.; Mary Ellen O'Connell, "Affirming the Ban
on Harsh Interrogation," 66 *Ohio State Law Journal* 1231
(2005); Philippe Sands, "The Green Light," *Vanity Fair*, May
2008, p. 218.

12. Scott Shane, "A Firsthand Experience Before Decision on
Torture," *New York Times*, November 7, 2007, p. A22. See Mark
Benjamin, "Waterboarding for Dummies," *Salon.com*, March
9, 2010, at www.salon.com/news/feature/2010/03/09/water
boarding_for_dummies. "Interrogators pumped detainees full
of so much water that the CIA turned to a special saline solution to minimize the risk of death. . . ."

13. In approving a memo from William J. Haynes, General
Counsel, Rumsfeld included a handwritten note: "However, I

stand for 8–10 hours a day. Why is standing limited to 4 hours? D.R." *The Torture Papers*, Greenberg and Dratel, eds. p. 237.

14. Some of these techniques are gathered in international legislation under the rubric "cruel, inhumane or degrading" treatment. See O'Connell, "Affirming the Ban on Harsh Interrogation," 1247–55.

15. Article 25 of the Geneva Convention Relative to the Treatment of Prisoners of War, August 12, 1949, United Nations, Treaty Series, vol. 75, p. 135 ("Third Geneva Convention"), requires that prisoners of war be housed in conditions "as favourable as those for the forces of the Detaining Power who are billeted in the same area." They must also have sufficient daily food rations and clothing (Articles 26–27), and medical inspections at least once a month (Article 31). Headquarters, Department of the Army, *Field Manual 2–22.3 (FM 34–52): Human Intelligence Collector Operations* (2006), available at http://www .army.mil/institution/armypublicaffairs/pdf/fm2-22-3.pdf, details the limits of acceptable interrogation tactics (ch. 8). For an excellent survey, see William Ranney Levi, "Interrogation's Law," 118 *Yale Law Journal* 1434 (2009).

16. Jean Amery's *At the Mind's Limits: Contemplations by a Survivor of Auschwitz and Its Realities*, Sydney Rosenfeld and Stella P. Rosenfeld, trans. (London: Granta Books, 1999) is a searing personal account of being tortured by the Gestapo. We use the word *spirit* because *mind* seems too specific and rational a capacity. We mean to include the ability not only to calculate but also to will, to desire, to imagine, to decide. In reflecting on this subject we have learned immeasurably from Elaine Scarry's lyrical work *The Body in Pain* and from David Sussman,

"What's Wrong with Torture?" *Philosophy and Public Affairs*, vol. 33 (2005), p. 1. See generally Seumas Miller, "Torture," in *The Stanford Encyclopedia of Philosophy*, Edward N. Zalta, ed. (Stanford, CA: Metaphysics Research Lab, Center for the Study of Language and Information, Stanford University, 2008), available at http://plato.stanford.edu/entries/torture/.

17. In this, pain is like disgust, which also seeks to compel us to avoidance whether we want it to or not. See William Ian Miller, *The Anatomy of Disgust* (Cambridge, MA: Harvard University Press, 1997), and Martha C. Nussbaum, *Hiding from Humanity: Disgust, Shame, and the Law* (Princeton: Princeton University Press, 2004).

18. Department of the Army, *Field Manual 2–22.3*, Para. 8–21 (2006).

19. See note 12 in "Absolutely Wrong" chapter.

20. For more discussion of the soldiers, photos, and the operation of the prison, see Philip Gourevitch and Errol Morris, *The Ballad of Abu Ghraib* (London: Penguin Books, 2008).

21. See the 2004 report of the official Article 15–6 military inquiry: Major General Antonio M. Taguba, *Article 15–6 Investigation of 800th Military Police Brigade* (no publisher, 2004). Link available at www.fas.org/irp/agnecy.dod.

22. *Rochin v. California*, 342 U.S. 165 (1952) (Frankfurter, J). Read more at http://law.jrank.org/pages/10268/Shock-Conscience-Test.html#ixzz0PllBxj4G.

23. *Winston v. Lee*, 470 U.S. 753 (1985). Winston did not invoke the "shocks the conscience" standard—it was decided as an unreasonable search, rather than as a violation of due process.

24. John H. Langbein, *Torture and the Law of Proof: Europe and*

England in the Ancien Régime (Chicago: University of Chicago Press, 2006).

25. Wars of aggression were determined to be crimes in the Nuremberg trials. See also "Definition of Aggression," *Resolutions Adopted by the General Assembly during Its Twenty-ninth Session*, United Nations Resolution 3314 (XXIX) (December 14, 1974). Aggression has also been made a crime under the Rome Statute of the International Criminal Court (Article 5), although so far it remains undefined.

26. Quoted in Robert F. Kennedy Jr., "America's Anti-Torture Tradition," *Los Angeles Times*, December 17, 2005.

27. The 1899 Hague Conventions first prohibited the use of expanding bullets and poisonous gases. July 29, 1899, Consolidated Treaty Series, vol. 187, p. 429. See also "Protocol for the Prohibition of the Use in War of Asphyxiating, Poisonous or Other Gases, and of Bacteriological Methods of Warfare," June 17, 1925, United States Treaties and Other International Agreements, vol. 26, p. 571 ("Geneva Protocol"), and the prohibitions discussed in "Exploding Bullets," ch. 26 in International Committee of the Red Cross, *Customary International Humanitarian Law: Rules* (Cambridge: Cambridge University Press, 2005), pp. 272–74 (discussing the evolution of a norm that originated in the St. Petersburg Declaration of 1868).

28. "Protocol Additional to the Geneva Conventions of 12 August 1949, and relating to the Protection of Victims of International Armed Conflicts," June 8, 1977, United Nations Treaty Series, vol. 1125, p. 3. Part 4 addresses prohibitions on attacks on civilians. Article 48 states, "In order to ensure respect for and

protection of the civilian population and civilian objects, the Parties to the conflict shall at all times distinguish between the civilian population and combatants and between civilian objects and military objectives and accordingly shall direct their operations only against military objectives." The full texts of these declarations and treaties are available in *Documents on the Laws of War*, Adam Roberts and Richard Guelff, eds. (New York: Oxford University Press, 2000).

29. Hugo Grotius was one of the earliest modern thinkers to make a distinction between combatants and noncombatants, in *De Jure Belli ac Pacis* [1625] Francis W. Kelsey, trans. (Buffalo, NY: William S. Hein, 1995), bk. 3. See also Emmerich Vattel, *The Law of Nations, or the Principles of Natural Law Applied to the Conduct and to the Affairs of Nations and of Sovereigns* [1758], trans. Charles G. Fenwick (Washington: Carnegie Institute, 1916), bk. 3, ch. 8, sects. 145–56, and the discussion of Kant's distinction between combatants and noncombatants in Brian Orend, *War and International Justice: A Kantian Perspective* (Waterloo, Ontario, Canada: Wilfrid Laurier University Press, 2000), pp. 50–60.

30. See, generally, Andrew J. Rotter, *Hiroshima: The World's Bomb* (Oxford: Oxford University Press, 2008).

31. Michael Walzer, in a chapter titled "Noncombatant Immunity and Military Necessity," discusses the balancing calculations inherent in these types of situations, in his *Just and Unjust Wars: A Moral Argument with Historical Illustrations* (New York: Basic Books, 1977). See also Thomas Hurka, "Proportionality in the Morality of War," *Philosophy and Public Affairs*, vol. 33 (2005), p. 34. See, generally, Gabriella Blum, "The Laws of

War and the Lesser Evil," 35 *Yale Journal of International Law* (forthcoming 2010).

32. Franz Kafka, "In The Penal Colony," in *The Metamorphosis and Other Stories* [1919], Stanley Appelbaum, trans. (New York: Dover, 1996), p. 53.

33. The Supreme Court has described a properly administered lethal injection as humane and painless. *Baze v. Rees*, 553 U.S. 35 (2008).

34. Immanuel Kant, in *The Metaphysics of Morals* [1797], Mary Gregor, trans. (Cambridge: Cambridge University Press, 1996), p. 107, argues that capital punishment should be carried out even by a society about to disband. Professors Cass R. Sunstein and Adrian Vermeule have offered the more usual defense of the death penalty: that it has been shown to save lives by its deterrent effect. This is a variant of the argument that it is justified to kill some in order to save more—especially as the perpetrator has been definitively found guilty of murder by fair procedures. See their article "Is Capital Punishment Morally Required? Acts Omissions and Life-Life Tradeoffs," 58 *Stanford Law Review* 703 (2006).

35. "Definition of Democracy," in *The Collected Works of Abraham Lincoln*, Basler, ed., p. 532. See also Hegel's dialectic of master and slave in which the master is shown to devalue his own person by how he treats humanity in the person of the slave. G. W. F. Hegel, *The Phenomenology of Mind*, J. B. Bailie, trans., rev. 2nd ed. (London: Allen and Unwin, 1949) (1807), pp. 228–40.

THE BIG EAR

1. James Bamford, "Who's in Big Brother's Database" [reviewing Matthew M. Aid, *The Secret Sentry: The Untold History of the National Security Agency*], *New York Review of Books*, November 5, 2009, pp. 29–31.

2. See, for example, Charlie Savage, "Loosening of F.B.I. Rules Stirs Privacy Concerns" New York Times, October 29, 2009, p. A1.

3. See Technology and Privacy Advisory Committee, U.S. Department of Defense, *Safeguarding Privacy in the Fight against Terrorism: The Report of the Technology and Privacy Advisory Committee* (March 1, 2004), pp. 33–35, available at http://www .cdt.org/security/usapatriot/20040300tapac.pdf. For a comprehensive review of the program and issues of privacy generally, see Peter Galison and Martha Minow, "Our Privacy, Ourselves in the Age of Technological Intrusions," in *Human Rights in the "War on Terror*," Richard Wilson, ed. (Cambridge: Cambridge University Press, 2005).

4. In his confirmation hearing, Leon Panetta stated that if he felt a situation required procedures beyond those being used, he "would not hesitate to go to the president of the United States and request whatever additional authority [he] would need." Mark Mazzetti, "Panetta Open to Tougher Methods in Some C.I.A. Interrogation," *New York Times*, February 6, 2009, p. A 14. For the Abdulmutallab case and the resistance to millimeter wave scanners, see Eric Lipton and Scott Shane, "Questions Why Suspect Wasn't Stopped," *New York Times*, December 27,

2009, available online at http://www.nytimes.com/2009/12/28/us/28terror.html?ref=us, and Kenneth Chang, "Explosive on Flight 253 Is among Most Powerful," *New York Times*, December 28, 2009, available online at http://www.nytimes.com/2009/12/28/us/28explosives.html?ref=us. For al Qaeda's use of body cavities to carry explosive devices, see Sheila MacVicar, "Al Qaeda Bombers Learn from Drug Smugglers," *CBS Evening News*, September 28, 2008, available online at http://www.cbsnews.com/stories/2009/09/28/eveningnews/main5347847.shtml.

5. *Olmstead v. United States*, 277 U.S. 438, 478 (1928) (Brandeis, J., dissenting).

6. See note 1 in "Introduction."

7. See Michelangelo's *The Drunkenness of Noah* in the Sistine Chapel, shown at the head of this chapter and available at www.abcgallery.com/M/michaelangelo/michaelangelo43.html.

8. The two motivations might merge. A person might want to appear rich in order to perpetrate a fraud on others, or poor in order to avoid being dunned for charity by poorer friends and relatives.

9. St. Augustine, *The City of God*, Marcus Dods, trans. (New York: Modern Library, 1993) bk. 14, ch.18.

10. *Dennis v. US*, 341 U.S. 494, 574, 577 (1951) (Jackson, J., concurring) (The law of conspiracy is the government's chief weapon in combating "permanently organized, well-financed, semi-secret and highly disciplined political organizations").

11. Langbein, *Torture and the Law of Proof.*

12. Blackstone's *Commentaries on the Laws of England*, vol. 2, Wayne Morrison, ed. (London: Cavendish, 2001), sect. 76 (1)

(1765–1769), p. 61. This imagining had to be accompanied by some "overt act," often in itself harmless or trivial.

13. The Fifth Amendment reads, "No person . . . shall be compelled in any criminal case to be a witness against himself."

14. *Fisher v. United States*, 425 U.S. 391, 409 (1976) (describing the "clear statements of this Court that under appropriate safeguards private incriminating statements of an accused may be overheard and used in evidence, if they are not compelled at the time they were uttered"); *Oregon v. Elstad*, 470 U.S. 298, 305 (1985) (noting the Fifth Amendment protections do not extend to "moral and psychological pressures to confess emanating from sources other than official coercion"); *United States v. Washington*, 431 U.S. 181, 187 (1977) ("Absent some officially coerced self-accusation, the Fifth Amendment privilege is not violated by even the most damning admissions").

15. Erving Goffman's *Presentation of Self in Everyday Life* (Garden City, NY: Doubleday, 1959) is the classic text that illustrates and analyzes the phenomena we describe in these paragraphs.

16. Max Beerbohm, *The Happy Hypocrite: A Fairy Tale for Tired Men* (New York: John Lane, 1922).

17. Against this intrinsic value Richard Posner pointed out the costs of excessive regard for the claim of persons to keep private information about themselves not just from officials but from the public at large. He even saw value in gossip and general unmotivated curiosity about the personal lives of others. Start with gossip and scandal: accounts of the habits and doings of the rich, the famous, the notorious, and even ordinary persons teach lessons in living; they broadcast the possibilities that are (or are not) open to us and that we might otherwise

not have imagined. In this sense scandal and gossip share an enlightening and liberating function with literature. This liberty to pierce privacy in order to learn what our social world is really like, to discover who we might be and who our partners in humanity really are, is the mirror image of the liberating function of privacy that allows us to (try to) become whomever we choose. See his article "The Right of Privacy," 12 *Georgia Law Review* 393 (1978).

18. Charles Fried, "Privacy: A Rational Context," in *An Anatomy of Values: Problems of Personal and Social Choice* (Cambridge: Harvard University Press, 1970); "Privacy," 77 *Yale Law Journal* 475 (1968).

19. Dershowitz, *Why Terrorism Works.*

20. See Daniel J. Solove, *Understanding Privacy* (Cambridge, MA: Harvard University Press, 2008); Galison and Minow, "Our Privacy, Ourselves in the Age of Technological Intrusions," pp. 277–84.

21. *Kyllo v. United States*, 533 U.S. 27 (2001).

22. The case is analyzed in detail and with great good humor by Jeannie Suk, *At Home in the Law: How the Domestic Violence Revolution Is Transforming Privacy* (New Haven: Yale University Press, 2009), ch. 5. She chose just those quotes from the decision.

23. *Katz v. United States* 389 U.S. 347 (1967).

24. Ibid., 361 (internal citations omitted).

25. Jed Rubenfeld has argued that the justifications for the "expectations-of-privacy analysis" leave the Fourth Amendment self-validating, indeterminate, or hollow. "The End of Privacy," 61 *Stanford Law Review* 101, 105–15 (2008).

26. Kate Summerscale, *The Suspicions of Mr. Whicher* (New York: Walker, 2008), p. 51.

27. "An intimate acquaintance with the refined customs and highest tones of society insures harmony in its conduct, while ignorance of them inevitably produces discords and confusion. Fortunate are those who were born in an atmosphere of intelligent refinement, because mistakes to them are almost impossible. . . . As to the unfortunates who have been reared at remote distances from the centers of civilization, there is nothing left for them to do but to make a careful study of unquestionable authority in those matters of etiquette which prevail among the most refined people." Abby Buchanan Longstreet, *Social Etiquette of New York* (New York: Appleton, 1892), pp. 7–8.

    "It would be absurd to suppose that those persons who constitute the upper ranks of the middle classes in London are ignorant of the regulations here laid down; but in the country, (especially in the mercantile districts,) where the tone of society is altogether lower, it is far otherwise, although country people may not feel inclined to *acknowledge* what is, nevertheless, strictly true." Charles William Day, *Hints on Etiquette and the Usages of Society; with a Glance at Bad Habits* (Boston: William D. Ticknor, 1844), p. 8.

    "There are deeper matters than these for which society is constituted; but society would be too busy arranging the minor details to attend to the big things, if order were not observed." A woman of fashion, *Etiquette for Americans* (New York: Herbert S. Stone, 1898), p. 13.

28. Catherine Yang, "The State of Surveillance," *BusinessWeek*, August 8, 2005, p. 52. (Britain has four million video cameras

monitoring public spaces; London has over half a million); New York Civil Liberties Union, "Who's Watching? Video Camera Surveillance in New York City and the Need for Public Oversight" (2006), available at http://www.nyclu .org/pdfs/surveillance_cams_report_121306.pdf (discussing the proliferation of surveillance cameras in New York City in the past decade); Charlie Savage, "U.S. Doles Out Millions for Street Cameras," *Boston Globe*, August 12, 2007, p. A1 (describing the distribution of federal money to fund local governments to purchase video networks).

NO BEGINNING OR NO END

1. Post 9/11, the threats culled from various intelligence reports were presented together in a daily "Threat Matrix." See Jack Goldsmith, *The Terror Presidency: Law and Judgment inside the Bush Administration* (New York: W.W. Norton, 2007), pp. 71–76; and Mayer, *The Dark Side*, pp. 5, 55. Despite the flood of threat reports, the government "ha[d] little 'actionable intelligence' about who [was] going to hit us, or where, or when," which only heightened the fear and anxiety. See Goldsmith, *The Terror Presidency*, p. 73. George Tenet, the director of the CIA at the time, wrote in his memoir, "We recognized that the matrix was a blunt instrument. You could drive yourself crazy believing all or even half of what was in it. It was exceptionally useful, however, and an unprecedented mechanism for systematically organizing, tracking, validating, cross-checking, and debunking the voluminous amount of threat data flowing

into the intelligence community." *At the Center of the Storm: My Years at the CIA* (New York: HarperCollins, 2007), p. 232.

2. The Continuity of Government Commission was established in the fall of 2002 as a joint project of the American Enterprise Institute and the Brookings Institution. It has issued two reports—a January 2003 report on the continuity of Congress and a July 2009 report on presidential succession. See www .continuityofgovernment.org (last visited November 30, 2009).

3. Address to Special Session of Congress (July 4, 1861) in *The Collected Works of Abraham Lincoln*, Basler, ed., pp. 421, 430.

4. *Ex Parte Merryman*, 17 F. Cas. 144 (C.C.D.Md. 1861).

5. *Ex Parte Milligan*, 71 U.S. 2 (1866). See, generally, John Yoo, "*Merryman* and *Milligan* (and *McCardle*)," 34 *Journal of Supreme Court History* 243 (2009). Justice Davis went on to explain: "Wicked men, ambitious of power, with hatred of liberty and contempt of law, may fill the place once occupied by Washington and Lincoln; and if this right is conceded, and the calamities of war again befall us, the dangers to human liberty are frightful to contemplate." *Ex Parte Milligan*, 216.

6. The classic sources for this episode are Spencer Tucker and Frank Reuter, *Injured Honor: The Chesapeake-Leopard Affair, June 22, 1807* (Annapolis: Naval Institute Press, 1996), and Henry Adams's *The Formative Years; A History of the United States during the Administrations of Jefferson and Madison* (London: Collins, 1948).

7. Thomas Jefferson, Letter to John B. Colvin, in *Social and Political Philosophy: Readings from Plato to Gandhi*, John Somerville and Ronald E. Santoni, eds. (New York: Anchor Books, 1963), p. 278.

8. The authorization for interrogation is set out in an August 1, 2002, opinion of the Justice Department's Office of Legal Counsel. The opinion concluded that "certain acts may be cruel, inhuman, or degrading, but still not produce pain and suffering of the requisite intensity to fall within Section 2340A's proscription against torture." The memo became infamous for its conclusion that torture requires the victim to suffer pain "of an intensity akin to that which accompanies serious physical injury such as death or organ failure." Bybee Memo, in *The Torture Papers*, Greenberg and Dratel, eds., pp. 172–217. The 2002 memorandum was withdrawn in 2004 and replaced by a Memorandum from Daniel Levin, Acting Assistant Attorney General, Office of Legal Counsel, to James B. Comey, Deputy Attorney General, U.S. Department of Justice (December 30, 2004), "Re: Legal Standards Applicable under 18 U.S.C. §§ 2340–2340A," available at http://www.usdoj.gov/olc/18usc23402340a2.htm.

9. 50 U.S.C. 1811 (2000).

10. The Foreign Intelligence Security Act (FISA) provides that a judge should approve a surveillance order if there is probable cause to believe that "the target of the electronic surveillance is a foreign power or agent of a foreign power and each of the facilities or places at which the electronic surveillance is directed is being used, or is about to be used, by a foreign power or an agent of a foreign power." Ibid., 1805. For an exchange of opinions between those who supported and opposed the wiretapping program, see 81 *Indiana Law Journal* (2006).

11. In 2003 when Jack Goldsmith, the new head of the Office

of Legal Counsel, reviewed the opinions of his predecessor in office, he found this claim excessive. Instead he limited it to the commander in chief's traditional powers to monitor enemy "signals intelligence" in wartime, arguing that the 2001 Authorization of Use of Military Force (AUMF) in effect repealed aspects of FISA. But even this permission was not sufficient to cover a number of unspecified intelligence-gathering practices that the president was determined to continue. See Goldsmith, *The Terror Presidency*, pp. 144–62 (describing Goldsmith's experience rescinding opinions), and pp. 180–84 (describing his experience with FISA); and the *Unclassified Report on the President's Surveillance Program, 10 July 2009*, prepared by the Offices of Inspectors General of the Department of Defense, Department of Justice, Central Intelligence Agency, National Security Agency, and Office of the Director of National Intelligence, pp. 19–30, available at http://www.globalsecurity.org/intell/library/reports/2009/psp-oigs_090710.pdf.

12. Bybee Memo (see note 8), 204–5 (internal citations omitted).

13. *Youngstown Sheet & Tube Co. v. Sawyer*, 343 U.S. 579, at 644 (1952) (Jackson, J. concurring). It is on the basis of Jackson's distinction that one of us defended the use of military commissions to determine the status and punish the crimes of enemy combatants. See Brief *Amicus Curiae* of Law Professors et al. in *Rasul v. Bush*, 542 U.S. 466 (2004) (No. 03–334), submitted by Ruth Wedgwood, Charles Fried, and Max Kampelman, serving as counsel for *amicus curiae*.

14. Stephen Breyer, *Making Our Democracy Work: A Judge's View* (New York: Alfred A. Knopf, 2010).

15. See J. A. F. Orbaan, *Sixtine Rome* (New York: Baker & Taylor, 1911), pp. 164–65. Justice David Souter told this story at a Law Day talk at Harvard in 2008.

16. Stephanie Ebbert, "In Rush-Hour Labor, Ticket Delivered," *Boston Globe*, December 4, 2008, at http://www.boston.com/news/local/massachusetts/articles/2008/12/04/in_rush_hour_labor_ticket_delivered/, accessed October 25, 2009.

17. Aristotle, *Nicomachean Ethics*, H. Rackham, trans. (Cambridge, MA: Harvard University Press, 1982), 5.10, 1137b, pp. 315, 317; translation amended by G. Fried.

18. Ibid., I.3, 1094b13, p.7.

19. Ibid., 5.6, 1134a.35–1134b1, p. 293; translation amended by G. Fried. A variant Greek manuscript has *logon* (reason) for *nomon* (law). "In Rome, . . . in emergencies, a single dictator with broader powers could be created, yet even the dictator's powers were hedged about with safeguards. . . . The sources are somewhat ambiguous about the length of the dictator's term, but most suggest a six-month limitation, roughly the length of the campaigning season. Even within that period, the dictator's powers lapsed when a designated task was accomplished." Adrian Vermeule, "Intermittent Institutions," Harvard Public Law Working Paper No. 10-13, January 25, 2010, available at http://papers.ssrn.com/sol3/papers.cfm?abstract_id=1542104 (2010), citing T. Corey Brennan, "Power and Process under the Republican 'Constitution,' " in *The Cambridge Companion to the Roman Republic*, Harriet I. Flower, ed. (Cambridge: Cambridge University Press, 2004), pp. 31, 42.

20. Robert Bolt, *A Man for All Seasons: A Play in Two Acts* (New York: Random House, 1962), p. 66.

21. American Law Institute, Model Penal Code, sect. 3.02 (1985). This is an unofficial compendium of what are thought to be the best provisions of many American legal codes. The section continues: "and (b) neither the Code nor other law defining the offense provides exceptions or defenses dealing with the specific situation involved; and (c) a legislative purpose to exclude the justification claimed does not otherwise plainly appear. (2) When the actor was reckless or negligent in bringing about the situation requiring a choice of evils or in appraising the necessity for his conduct, the justification afforded by this section is unavailable in a prosecution for any offense for which recklessness or negligence, as the case may be, suffices to establish culpability."

22. Aristotle, *The Politics*, C. D. C. Reeve, trans. (Cambridge: Hackett, 1998), bk. 3, ch. 17, 1288a14–18, p. 99.

23. Plato, *The Republic*, Tom Griffin, trans. (Cambridge: Cambridge University Press, 2001), bk. 6, 488a–489b, p. 191.

24. Michael Wilson, "Flight 1549 Pilot Tells of Terror and Intense Focus," *New York Times*, February 8, 2009, p. A19; J. Lynn Lunsford, "Praise Heaped on Veteran Airman for Pulling Off Rare Feat," *Wall Street Journal*, January 16, 2009, p. A3.

25. Aristotle, *Politics*, bk. 3, ch. 15, 1286a7–20, p. 94.

26. Ibid., 1286a7–8, p. 94.

27. John Locke, *Two Treatises of Government* [1690] Peter Laslett ed., 2nd ed. (London: Cambridge University Press, 1967), p. 391.

28. Ibid., p. 393.

29. Ibid.

30. Ibid., p. 396.

31. "For when their Successors, managing the Government with different Thoughts, would draw the Actions of those good Rulers into Precedent, and make them the Standard of their Prerogative, as if what had been done only for the good of the People, was a right in them to do, for the harm of the People, if they so pleased." (sect. 166). Ibid.

32. *Youngstown Sheet & Tube Co. v. Sawyer*, 343 U.S. 579, 653 (1952) (Jackson, J. concurring). The full passage in question is worth quoting:

> The appeal, however, that we declare the existence of inherent powers ex necessitate to meet an emergency asks us to do what many think would be wise, although it is something the forefathers omitted.
>
> Germany, after the First World War, framed the Weimar Constitution, designed to secure her liberties in the Western tradition. However, the President of the Republic, without concurrence of the Reichstag, was empowered temporarily to suspend any or all individual rights if public safety and order were seriously disturbed or endangered. This proved a temptation to every government, whatever its shade of opinion, and in 13 years suspension of rights was invoked on more than 250 occasions. Finally, Hitler persuaded President Von Hindenburg to suspend all such rights, and they were never restored.
>
> In view of the ease, expedition and safety with which Congress can grant and has granted large emergency powers, certainly ample to embrace this crisis, I am

quite unimpressed with the argument that we should affirm possession of them without statute. Such power either has no beginning or it has no end. If it exists, it need submit to no legal restraint. I am not alarmed that it would plunge us straightway into dictatorship, but it is at least a step in that wrong direction.

33. Jefferson, Letter to John B. Colvin.

LEARNING NOT TO BE GOOD

1. The tension between private morality and public responsibility has been much discussed. For Michael Walzer, the dilemma of dirty hands is that moral beliefs must sometimes be overridden, "a painful process which forces a man to weigh the wrong he is willing to do in order to do right." The dilemma may exist in private life, "[b]ut the issue is posed most dramatically in politics for the three reasons that make political life the kind of life it is, because we claim to act for others but also serve ourselves, rule over others, and use violence against them." See his article "Political Action: The Problem of Dirty Hands," *Philosophy and Public Affairs*, vol. 2 (1973), pp. 160, 174. Max Weber describes "the abysmal contrast between conduct that follows the maxim of an ethic of ultimate ends—that is, in religious terms, 'The Christian does rightly and leaves the results with the Lord'— and conduct that follows the maxim of an ethic of responsibility, in which case one has to give an account of the foreseeable results of one's actions." Despite recognizing that these are not

absolute contrasts, he nonetheless recognizes them as framing an ethical paradox: "He who seeks the salvation of his soul, of his own and of others, should not seek it along the avenue of politics." See his "Politics as a Vocation," in *From Max Weber: Essays in Sociology*, H. H. Gerth and C. Wright Mills, trans. (New York: Oxford University Press, 1946), pp. 126, 120. Thomas Nagel has recognized a similar distinction as relevant to distinguishing personal and public obligations: the distinction between "concern with what will happen and concern with what one is doing." Although he also recognizes that public office carries with it "special obligations" that reduce a politician's right to consider personal or more general moral obligations, he defines limits on a politician's obligations in terms of public morality. See Nagel's "Ruthlessness in Public Life," in *Mortal Questions* (New York: Cambridge University Press, 1979), pp. 83, 89. János Kis, *Politics as a Moral Problem* (Budapest and New York: Central European University Press, 2008), especially chapters 8 and 9, combines a scholar's survey of these writings with a philosopher's probing, even relentless, analysis of the problem. The work is exemplary.

2. Aristotle, *Politics*, bk. 1. Aristotle states, "A complete community . . . comes to be for the sake of living, but it remains in existence for the sake of living well." Ibid., ch. 2, 1252b28–29, p. 3.

3. Five days after 9/11, Vice President Cheney described the administration's response as a move to the "the dark side." He said, "We've got to spend time in the shadows in the intelligence world. A lot of what needs to be done here will have to be done quietly, without any discussion, using sources

and methods that are available to our intelligence agencies." Mayer, *The Dark Side*, p. 9. Other members of the administration echoed this idea: Cofer Black, the director of the CIA's Counterterrorist Center, stated, "[A]fter 9/11 the gloves come off." Joint House/Senate Intelligence Committee Hearing, Testimony of Cofer Black (September 26, 2002).

4. See note 1 in "No Beginning or No End" chapter.

5. Niccolo Machiavelli, *The Prince*, [1532] Mark Musa, trans., (New York: St. Martin's Press, 1964), ch. 15, p. 127.

6. Walzer, "Political Action," p. 160.

7. Ibid., p. 161.

8. Ibid.

9. Imagining a politician faced with making a dishonest deal to win an election, Walzer argues, "[a]ssuming that this particular election ought to be won, it is clear, I think, that . . . disparagement is justified. If the candidate didn't want to get his hands dirty, he should have stayed at home; if he can't stand the heat, he should get out of the kitchen, and so on." "Political Action," p. 165.

10. Weber, "Politics as a Vocation," p. 126.

11. In his book, *The Real War*, (London: Sidgwick Jackson, 1980), Nixon's Machiavellian streak is apparent: "World leadership requires something in many ways alien to the American cast of mind. It requires placing limits on idealism, compromising with reality, at times matching duplicity with duplicity, and even brutality with brutality," (p. 69). See also "Nation: The Real Nixon," *Time*, June 9, 1980, available at http://www.time.com/time/magazine/article/0,9171,952649,00.html (elaborating on Nixon's Machiavellian techniques). See, generally,

Stephen E. Ambrose, *Nixon* (New York: Simon & Schuster, 1987–91).

12. Here is what the Supreme Court of Israel had to say on the subject: "We are aware that this decision [limiting possible interrogation techniques] does not ease dealing with that reality [of terrible situations facing the security forces]. This is the destiny of democracy, as not all means are acceptable to it, and not all practices employed by its enemies are open before it. Although, a democracy must often fight with one hand tied behind its back, it nonetheless has the upper hand. Preserving the Rule of Law and recognition of an individual's liberty constitutes an important component of its understanding of security. At the end of the day, they strengthen its spirit and its strength and allow it to overcome its difficulties."

Justice Aharon Barak, Israeli Supreme Court, *Public Committee Against Torture in Israel v. Israel*, 53(4) P.D. 817, at p. 845.

13. See Sidney Blumenthal, "Meek, Mild and Menacing," *Salon.com*, January 12, 2006, at www.salon.com/opinion /blumenthal/2006/01/12/alito_bush/.

14. "The Presidency: The World of Harry Truman," *Time*, January 8, 1973); *Wounded Titans: American Presidents and the Perils of Power*, Max Lerner, ed. (New York: Arcade, 1996), p. 213. Some have speculated that Truman's other statements—and even the very vehemence with which he asserted his lack of doubt— suggest "an element of insecurity concerning the decision." See Andrew J. Rotter, *Hiroshima: The World's Bomb* (Oxford: Oxford University Press, 2008), p. 233.

15. Harvey C. Mansfield, in "The Case for the Strong Executive,"

Claremont Review of Books, vol. 7, no. 2 (Spring 2007), pp. 21–24, as well as in his book on Machiavelli, *Taming the Prince* (London: Collier Macmillan, 1989), recognizes this point but appears to celebrate rather than regret it.

16. To the extent that the argument is a utilitarian one, the actor is left unable even to consider his moral intuitions. Bernard Williams describes the situation of "Jim," a man faced with a classic utilitarian dilemma of killing one man to save many. Williams argues that the utilitarian's appeal for Jim to overcome his "self-indulgent squeamishness" asks Jim to view his emotional experience of the act's wrongness not as a moral question, but instead merely as an unpleasant experience that should be given little weight. "The reason why the squeamishness appeal can be very unsettling, and one can be unnerved by the suggestion of self-indulgence in going against utilitarian considerations, is not that we are utilitarians who are uncertain what utilitarian value to attach to our moral feelings, but that we are partially at least not utilitarians, and cannot regard our moral feelings merely as objects of utilitarian value . . . to come to regard those feelings from a purely utilitarian point of view, that is to say, as happenings outside one's moral self, is to lose a sense of one's moral identity; to lose, in the most literal way, one's integrity." "A Critique of Utilitarianism," in *Utilitarianism: For and Against*, J. J. C Smart and Bernard Williams, eds. (Cambridge: Cambridge University Press, 1973), p. 98.

17. Compare, for example, Martin Luther King's *Letter from the Birmingham Jail* (San Francisco: Harper, 1994) with Vaclav Havel's 1989 address, "The Declaration of the Civic Forum by

Representative Vaclav Havel on Wenceslas Square," in Making the History of 1989, Item #509, available at http://chnm.gmu.edu/1989/items/show/509. King invokes the constitution and lawmaking processes in arguing for a moral responsibility to disobey unjust laws, whereas Havel rejects the system itself in declaring "the certainty that there is no return to the previous totalitarian system of government, which led our country to the brink of an absolute spiritual, moral, political, economic and ecological crisis."

18. *Brown v. Louisiana*, 383 U.S. 133 (1966).

19. Oren Gross, "The Prohibition on Torture and the Limits of Law," in *Torture: A Collection*, Levinson, ed. See also Gregory Fried, "By Law Unbound: Lessons on Executive Prerogative from Aristotle and Locke," Fourteenth Annual Conference for Core Texts and Courses, April 4, 2008.

20. FISA Amendments Act of 2008, Pub. L. No. 110–261, 122 Stat. 2436. The Supreme Court in *Ex Parte Milligan* did not so much deny this logic but rather declared for the future that Lincoln's original action had been illegal in the past. See note 4 in "No Beginning or No End" chapter.

21. The Decision of 1789 was an early debate in the House of Representatives dealing with the mechanisms for removing executive officers. Traditionally, the decision was seen as establishing that the president had full power to remove officers. In 1867, however, Congress passed the Tenure of Office Act, which prohibited the president from dismissing officeholders without the Senate's approval. President Johnson intentionally violated the Tenure of Office Act by discharging his secretary of war, leading to his impeachment. Just nineteen years

later, Congress repealed the act, and forty years after that the Supreme Court, in *Myers v. United States*, 272 U.S. 52 (1926), affirmed that the Tenure of Office Act was invalid. In *Myers*, the Court described the Decision of 1789, concluding, "[A]fter an examination of the record, that the vote was, and was intended to be, a legislative declaration that the power to remove officers appointed by the President and the Senate vested in the President alone, and until the Johnson impeachment trial in 1868 its meaning was not doubted, even by those who questioned its soundness." Ibid., p. 114. See, generally, William H. Rehnquist, *Grand Inquests: The Historic Impeachments of Justice Samuel Chase and President Andrew Johnson* (New York: Morrow, 1992), and Michael Les Benedict, *The Impeachment and Trial of Andrew Johnson* (New York: W. W. Norton, 1973).

22. Jefferson, Letter to Colvin, p. 279.

23. Gonzales appeared before the Senate Judiciary Committee to address the administration's warrantless domestic surveillance operations on February 6, 2006. Senate Judiciary Committee Hearing, Tesimony of Alberto Gonzales (February 6, 2006), available at http://fas.org/irp/congress/2006_hr/nsasurv.html. Several weeks later, he sent a letter clarifying his testimony. Charles Babington and Dan Eggen, "Gonzales Seeks To Clarify Testimony on Spying," *Washington Post*, March 1, 2006, p. A8.

24. Jack Goldsmith makes this case vividly, showing how the use of "lawfare" has come to intimidate governmental officials and how it may dissuade promising men and women from serving their country, given the reasonable fear that if they engage in important but controversial work, they could face financially

crushing legal action or even jail. See *The Terror Presidency*, pp. 53–70.

25. See note 3.

26. For example, the Civil Liberties Act of 1988 authorized payments for victims of the internment program and "acknowledged the fundamental injustice of the evacuation, relocation, and internment of United States citizens and permanent resident aliens of Japanese ancestry during World War II." 50 U.S.C. app. 1989 (2000).

27. Chris Hastings, "Churchill Wanted Hitler Sent to the Electric Chair," *Telegraph*, January 1, 2006, p. 12.

28. The Khmer Rouge prosecution was also a travesty. Millions dead, but only five indicted!

29. William Ranney Levi, "Interrogation's Law," 118 *Yale Law Journal* L.J.1434 (2009).

30. Ibid., 1466.

31. This was of course Goering's complaint at Nuremberg. See Gary Bass, *Stay the Hand of Vengeance* (Princeton: Princeton University Press, 2000), for a counterargument to Goering. See also Nir Eisikovits, "Transitional Justice," in the *Stanford Encyclopedia of Philosophy*, available online at http://plato.stanford.edu/entries/justice-transitional/.

32. See Gross, "The Prohibition of Torture and the Limits of Law," p. 242.

ACKNOWLEDGMENTS

Many friends and colleagues have offered advice and comments on some, even all of the chapters in this book. They have been very generous, so it is particularly urgent to insist that not only the opinions but also the mistakes are all our own. At Columbia Law School, where Charles was visiting professor during the 2008–2009 academic year, he profited from comments by Kent Greenawalt, Avery Katz, and Matthew Waxman, as well as participants in the law and philosophy colloquium there. At Harvard Law School, Gabriella Blum, Jack Goldsmith, and Jeannie Suk offered much help and encouragement. At Suffolk University, Nir Eisikovits was a constant friend and critic. We benefited from the research assistance of Asher Sered, a student at Swathmore, of Ryan Roberts at Lincoln Land Community College, and of Jarrod Abbott-Washburn and Brian Smith, students in Suffolk's graduate program in Ethics and Public Policy; in particular, we are grateful to the patient and diligent contributions of Kathryn Nielson, Harvard

Law School class of 2010. Claire Riley was a great help in preparing the final manuscript. Finally, we cannot overstate our gratitude to Bob Weil at W. W. Norton. His boundless enthusiasm encouraged us to work with joy and hope; his meticulous editing and his imaginative questions spurred our work to a higher level.

INDEX

ABOUT THE AUTHORS

Charles Fried is the Beneficial Professor of Law at Harvard Law School. Born in Prague in 1935, he fled with his family in 1939, first to England and then to the United States. Educated in public and private schools, he received his bachelor's degree from Princeton and law degrees from Oxford and Columbia Universities. After a clerkship on the Supreme Court with Justice John M. Harlan, he went to Harvard, where he has taught since 1961. He was solicitor general of the United States, the advocate for the United States in the Supreme Court during the second Reagan administration, and a justice of the Supreme Judicial Court of Massachusetts from 1995 to 1999. In addition to teaching and writing, he has litigated numerous issues as a private lawyer, including the constitutionality of flag desecration statutes for the American Civil Liberties Union, the proper courtroom use of scientific evidence, and whether the attack on the World Trade Center constituted one occurrence or two. He is the author of eight books on legal and philosophical subjects. His most recent book is *Modern Liberty and the Limits of Government* (Norton, 2006). In 1959 he married Anne Summerscale, whom he met while they were students in Oxford. They have two children and five grandchildren.

Gregory Fried is professor and chair of the Philosophy Department at Suffolk University, where he teaches ethics, political philosophy, and the history of philosophy. He received his BA from Harvard College and his PhD from the Committee on Social Thought at the University of Chicago, where he wrote a dissertation on Heidegger and politics under the direction of Leszek Kolakowski. He is the author of *Heidegger's Polemos* and the director of the Mirror of Race, an online project on race, photography, and American history. He is married to Christina Hardway, a developmental psychologist, and lives in Auburndale, Massachusetts, with their two children, Jonah and Eliza.